THINK AND GROW RICH

NAPOLEON HILL

Adapted for the 21st century reader and annotated by Richard Goddart.

The Ultimate Guide to Achieving

Powerful Personal Success

With Self-Coaching Workbook Tool

Second Edition

Copyright © Yana Golovanova 2019

Adaptation and notes: Richard Goddart

Napoleon Hill has asserted his rights to be identified as the author of this work in accordance with the Copyright, Designs and Patents Act 1988

The first edition of this book was published in Denmark by Saxo Publishing.

Contents

PREFACE

WHAT DO YOU WANT MOST?

*Is It Money, Fame, Power,
Contentment, Personality,
Peace of Mind, Happiness?*

The Thirteen Steps to Riches offer the shortest dependable philosophy of individual achievement.

This book conveys the experience of men of great wealth, who began at scratch, with nothing to give in return for riches except thoughts, ideas and organized plans. Here you have the entire philosophy of moneymaking. It describes WHAT TO DO, and also, HOW TO DO IT!

It presents complete instructions on how to sell your personal services.

It provides you with a perfect system of self-analysis that will readily disclose what has been standing between you and "the big money" in the past.

The book was inspired by Andrew Carnegie, after he had made his millions and retired.

Perhaps you do not need all that is to be found in the book, but you may need ONE IDEA, PLAN OR SUGGESTION to start you toward your goal. Somewhere in the book you will find this needed stimulus.

In this volume will be found the thirteen principles of moneymaking essential to every person who accumulates sufficient money to guarantee financial independence.

Riches cannot always be measured in money! Money and material things are essential for freedom of body and mind, but there are some who will feel that the greatest of all riches can be evaluated only in terms of lasting friendships, harmonious family relationships, sympathy and understanding between business associates, and introspective harmony which brings one peace of mind measurable only in spiritual values!

All who read, understand and apply this philosophy will be better prepared to attract and enjoy these higher estates which always have been and always will be denied to all except those who are ready for them.

Be prepared, therefore, when you expose yourself to the influence of this philosophy, to experience a CHANGED LIFE which may help you not only to negotiate your way through life with harmony and understanding, but also to prepare you for the accumulation of material riches in abundance.

Before beginning the book you will profit greatly if you recognize the fact that the book was not written to entertain. It is a textbook on individual achievement. It should be studied, digested, and meditated upon. A real student will not merely read this book, he will absorb its contents and make them his own. This philosophy will enable one to organize and apply the acquired knowledge, and convert it into useful service and adequate compensation without waste of time.

APPLYING THE MASTERMIND PRINCIPLE

The author discovered that successful people follow the habit of exchanging ideas, through what is commonly called conferences. When they had problems to be solved they sat down together and talked freely until they discovered, from their joint contribution of ideas, a plan that would serve their purpose.

You, who read this book, will get most out of it by putting into practice the Master Mind principle described in the book. This you can do by forming a study club, consisting of any desired number of people who are friendly and harmonious. The reading at the club should be done by someone who reads well and understands how to put color and feeling into the lines.

By following this plan every reader will get from its pages, not only the sum total of the best knowledge organized from the experiences of hundreds of successful men, but more important by far, he will tap new sources of knowledge in his own mind as well as acquire knowledge of priceless value FROM EVERY OTHER PERSON PRESENT.

CHAPTER 1
THE POWER OF THOUGHT

Thoughts are things, and powerful things, when they are mixed with definiteness of purpose, persistence, and a burning desire for their translation into riches or other objectives.

Life is strange, and often imponderable. Both the successes and the failures have their roots in simple experiences. Some experiences are commonplace and simple enough, yet they hold the answer to one's destiny in life, and therefore they are as important as life itself. But the one who has neither the time, nor the inclination to study failure in search of knowledge that may lead to success, can still learn the art of converting defeat into stepping stones to opportunity through the lessons taught in this summary.

The answer you may be seeking, to the questions which have caused you to ponder over the strangeness of life, may be found in your own mind, through some idea, plan, or purpose which may spring into your mind as you read.

One sound idea is all that one needs to achieve success.

The principles described in this book, contain the best, and the most practical of all that is known, concerning ways and means of creating and implementing **useful ideas**.

When riches begin to come they come so quickly, in such great abundance, that one wonders where they have been hiding during all those lean years.

This is an astounding statement, and all the more so, when we take into consideration the popular belief, that riches come only to those who work hard and long.

When you begin to THINK AND GROW RICH, you will observe that riches begin with a state of mind, with definiteness of purpose, with little or no hard work. You, and every other person, ought to be interested in knowing how to acquire that **state of mind** which will attract riches.

The business depression started in 1929, and continued on to an all time record of destruction, until sometime after President Roosevelt entered office. Then the depression began to fade into nothingness. Just as an electrician in a theatre raises the lights so gradually that darkness is transmuted into light before you realize it, so did the spell of fear in the minds of the people gradually fade away and become faith.

Observe very closely, as soon as you master the principles of this philosophy, and begin to follow the instructions for applying those principles, your financial status will begin to improve, and everything you touch will begin to transmute itself into an asset for your benefit. Impossible? Not at all!

One of the main weaknesses of mankind is the average man's familiarity with the word "impossible." He knows all the rules which will NOT work. He knows all the things which CANNOT be done. This book was written for those who seek the rules which have made others successful, and are willing to stake everything on those rules.

Success comes to those who become SUCCESS CONSCIOUS. Failure comes to those who indifferently allow themselves to become FAILURE CONSCIOUS. The object of this book is to help all who seek it, to learn the art of changing their minds from FAILURE CONSCIOUSNESS to SUCCESS CONSCIOUSNESS.

Be wary of some people's habit of measuring everything, and everyone, by their own impressions and beliefs. Some people believe that no one can THINK AND GROW RICH. They cannot think in terms of riches, because their thought habits have been steeped in poverty, want, misery, failure, and defeat. We refuse to believe that which we do not understand. We can foolishly believe that our own limitations are the proper measure of general limitations.

YOU ARE "THE MASTER OF YOUR FATE, THE CAPTAIN OF YOUR SOUL," BECAUSE...

When Henley wrote the prophetic lines, "I am the Master of my Fate, I am the Captain of my Soul," he should have informed us that we are the Masters of our Fate, the Captains of our Souls, because we have **the power to control our thoughts**.

The ether in which the Earth floats is a form of energy moving at an inconceivably high rate of vibration, and that ether is filled with a form of universal power which adapts itself to the nature of the thoughts we hold in our minds; and influences us, in natural ways, to transmute our thoughts into their physical equivalent.

This power makes no attempt to discriminate between destructive thoughts and constructive thoughts, and it will urge us to translate into physical reality thoughts of poverty, just as quickly as it will influence us to act upon thoughts of riches.

Our brains become magnetized with the dominating thoughts which we hold in our minds, and, by means with which no man is familiar, these "magnets" attract to us the forces, the people, and the circumstances of life which harmonize with the nature of our dominating thoughts. Before we can accumulate riches in great abundance, we must magnetize our minds with intense desire for riches, that we must become "money conscious" until the desire for money drives us to create definite plans for acquiring it.

Little by little, the truth has unfolded itself, until it now appears certain that the principles described in this book, hold the secret of mastery over our economic fate.

CHAPTER 2
DESIRE

THE STARTING POINT OF ALL ACHIEVEMENT

The First Step toward Riches

Note: you can be driven by other desires than accumulation of wealth: you can aspire to create a community, to get means to invest in a goal, or you can strive for knowledge and truth, and nevertheless, even if you don't feel a desire for money expressively, you can understand that anything that drives you is a desire. In this chapter you are invited to formulate your desires and to give them direction. More recent studies (i.e. described by Lynne McTaggart in "The Field") suggest that a moderate desire has better chances for its fulfillment.

Every human being who reaches the age of understanding of the purpose of money, wishes for it. Wishing will not bring riches. But desiring riches with a state of mind that becomes an obsession, then planning definite ways and means to acquire riches, and backing those plans with persistence which does not recognize failure, will bring riches. The method by which DESIRE for riches can be transmuted into its financial equivalent, consists of six definite, practical steps:

- ❑ First. Fix in your mind the exact amount of money you desire. It is not sufficient merely to say "I want plenty of money." Be definite as to the amount. (There is a psychological reason for definiteness which will be described in a subsequent chapter).
- ❑ Second. Determine exactly what you intend to give in return for the money you desire. (There is no such reality as "something for nothing.).
- ❑ Third. Establish a definite date when you intend to possess the money you desire.

❑ Fourth. Create a definite plan for carrying out your desire, and begin at once, whether you are ready or not, to put this plan into action.

❑ Fifth. Write out a clear, concise statement of the amount of money you intend to acquire, name the time limit for its acquisition, state what you intend to give in return for the money, and describe clearly the plan through which you intend to accumulate it.

❑ Sixth. Read your written statement aloud, twice daily, once just before retiring at night, and once after arising in the morning. AS YOU READ—SEE AND FEEL AND BELIEVE YOURSELF ALREADY IN POSSESSION OF THE MONEY.

It is important that you follow the instructions described in these six steps. It is especially important that you observe, and follow the instructions in the sixth paragraph. You may complain that it is impossible for you to "see yourself in possession of money" before you actually have it. Here is where a BURNING DESIRE will come to your aid. If you truly DESIRE money so keenly that your desire is an obsession, you will have no difficulty in convincing yourself that you will acquire it. The object is to want money, and to become so determined to have it that you CONVINCE yourself you will have it.

Only those who become "money conscious" ever accumulate great riches. "Money consciousness" means that the mind has become so thoroughly saturated with the DESIRE for money, that one can see one's self already in possession of it. To the uninitiated, who has not been schooled in the working principles of the human mind, these instructions may appear impractical.

These steps are not only essential for the accumulation of money, but necessary for the attainment of any definite goal. The steps call for no "hard labor." They call for no sacrifice. They do not require one to become ridiculous, or credulous. To apply them calls for no great amount of education. But the successful application of these six steps does call for sufficient imagination to enable one to see, and to understand, that accumulation of money cannot be left to chance, good fortune, and luck. One must realize that all who have accumulated great fortunes, first did a certain amount of dreaming, hoping, wishing, DESIRING, and PLANNING before they acquired money.

You may as well know, right here, that you can never have riches in great quantities, UNLESS you can work yourself into a white heat of DESIRE for money, and actually BELIEVE you will possess it.

You may as well know, also that every great leader, from the dawn of civilization down to the present, was a dreamer. Christianity is the greatest potential power in the world today, because its founder was an intense dreamer who had the vision and the imagination to see realities in their mental and spiritual form before they had been transmuted into physical form.

Never has there been so great an opportunity for practical dreamers as now exists. The rules of the race have changed, because we now live in a CHANGED WORLD that definitely favors the masses. We should be encouraged to know that this changed world in which we live is demanding new ideas, new ways of doing things, new leaders, new inventions, new methods of teaching, new methods of marketing, new books, new literature, new features for the radio, new ideas for moving pictures. Back of all this demand for new and better things, there is one quality which one must possess to win, and that is DEFINITENESS OF PURPOSE, the knowledge of what one wants, and a burning DESIRE to attain it.

This changed world requires practical dreamers who can, and will put their dreams into action. The practical dreamers have always been, and always will be the pattern-makers of civilization. We should remember that the real leaders of the world always have been men who harnessed, and put into practical use, the intangible, unseen forces of unborn opportunity, and have converted those forces, [or impulses of thought], into sky-scrapers, cities, factories, airplanes, automobiles, and every form of convenience that makes life more pleasant.

Tolerance, and an open mind are practical necessities of the dreamer of today. Those who are afraid of new ideas are doomed before they start. Never has there been a time more favorable to pioneers than the present. There is a vast business, financial, and industrial world to be remolded and redirected along new and better lines.

In planning to acquire your share of the riches, let no one influence you to scorn the dreamer. To win the big stakes in this changed world, you must catch the spirit of the great pioneers of the past, whose dreams have given to civilization all that it has of value, the spirit which serves as the life-blood of our own country—your opportunity and mine, to develop and market our talents.

"SUCCESS REQUIRES NO APOLOGIES, FAILURE PERMITS NO ALIBIS." If the thing you wish to do is right, and you believe in it, go ahead and do it! Put your dream across, and never mind what "they" say if you meet with temporary defeat, for "they," perhaps, do not know that EVERY FAILURE BRINGS WITH IT THE SEED OF AN EQUIVALENT SUCCESS.

The dreamers of today have tremendous opportunities. The world has become accustomed to new discoveries. Nay, it has shown a willingness to reward the dreamer who gives the world a new idea.

"The oak sleeps in the acorn. The bird waits in the egg, and in the highest vision of the soul, a waking angel stirs. DREAMS ARE THE SEEDLINGS OF REALITY."

Awake, arise, and assert yourself, you dreamers of the world. Your star is now in the ascendency. The world is filled with an abundance of OPPORTUNITY which the dreamers of the past never knew.

A BURNING DESIRE TO BE, AND TO DO is the starting point from which the dreamer must take off. Dreams are not born of indifference, laziness, or lack of ambition. The world no longer scoffs at the dreamer, nor calls him impractical.

Maybe you have been disappointed, maybe you have undergone defeat and have felt the great heart within you crushed until it bled. Take courage, for these experiences have tempered the spiritual metal of which you are made - they are assets of incomparable value. Remember, too, that all who succeed in life get off to a bad start, and pass through many heartbreaking struggles before they "arrive."

The turning point in the lives of those who succeed, usually comes at the moment of some crisis, through which they are introduced to their "other selves."

John Bunyan wrote the Pilgrim's Progress, which is among the finest of all English literature, after he had been confined in prison and sorely punished, because of his views on the subject of religion. Being FORCED, through misfortune, to become acquainted with his "other self," and to use his IMAGINATION, he discovered himself to be a great author instead of a miserable criminal and outcast.

Strange and varied are the ways of life, and stranger still are the ways of Infinite Intelligence, through which men are sometimes forced to undergo all sorts of punishment before discovering their own brains, and their own capacity to create useful ideas through imagination.

Disappointment over love affairs, generally has the effect of driving men to drink, and women to ruin; and this, because most people never learn the art of transmuting their strongest emotions into dreams of a constructive nature.

If you have the proper states of mind, and a working knowledge of the principles described, all else that you need will come to you, when you are READY for it. Let Emerson state the thought in these words:

"Every proverb, every book, every byword that belongs to thee for aid and comfort shall surely come home through open or winding

passages. Every friend whom not thy fantastic will, but the great and tender soul in thee craveth, shall lock thee in his embrace."

There is a difference between WISHING for a thing and being READY to receive it. No one is ready for a thing, until he believes he can acquire it. The state of mind must be BELIEF, not mere hope or wish. Open-mindedness is essential for belief. Closed minds do not inspire faith, courage, and belief. Remember, no more effort is required to aim high in life, to demand abundance and prosperity, than is required to accept misery and poverty.

Nothing is impossible to the person who backs DESIRE with enduring FAITH. Verily, a BURNING DESIRE has devious ways of transmuting itself into its physical equivalent. I believe in the power of DESIRE backed by FAITH, because I have seen this power lift men from lowly beginnings to places of power and wealth; I have seen it rob the grave of its victims; I have seen it serve as the medium by which men staged a comeback after having been defeated in a hundred different ways.

How can one harness and use the power of DESIRE? This has been answered through this, and the subsequent chapters of this book.

All achievement, no matter what may be its nature, or its purpose, must begin with an intense, BURNING DESIRE for something definite. Through some strange and powerful principle of "mental chemistry" which she has never divulged, Nature wraps up in the impulse of STRONG DESIRE "that something" which recognizes no such word as impossible, and accepts no such reality as failure.

CHAPTER 3
FAITH

VISUALIZATION OF, AND BELIEF IN ATTAINMENT OF DESIRE

The Second Step toward Riches

FAITH is the head chemist of the mind. When FAITH is blended with the vibration of thought, the subconscious mind instantly picks up the vibration, translates it into its spiritual equivalent, and transmits it to Infinite Intelligence, as in the case of prayer.

The emotions of FAITH, LOVE, and SEX are the most powerful of all the major positive emotions. When the three are blended, they have the effect of "coloring" the vibration of thought in such a way that it instantly reaches the subconscious mind, where it is changed into its spiritual equivalent, the only form that induces a response from Infinite Intelligence.

Love and faith are psychic; related to the spiritual side of man. Sex is purely biological, and related only to the physical. The mixing, or blending, of these three emotions has the effect of opening a direct line of communication between the finite, thinking mind of man, and Infinite Intelligence.

HOW TO DEVELOP FAITH

There comes, now, a statement which will give a better understanding of the importance the principle of auto-suggestion assumes in the transmutation of desire into its physical equivalent; namely: FAITH is a state of mind which may be induced, or created, by affirmation or repeated instructions to the subconscious mind, through the principle of auto-suggestion.

As an illustration, consider the purpose for which you are, presumably, reading this book. The object is, naturally, to acquire the ability to transmute the intangible thought impulse of DESIRE into its physical counterpart. By following the instructions laid down in the chapters on auto-suggestion, and the subconscious mind, as summarized in the chapter on auto-suggestion, you may CONVINCE the subconscious mind that you believe you will receive that for which you ask, and it will act upon that belief, which your subconscious mind passes back to you in the form of "FAITH," followed by definite plans for procuring that which you desire.

Faith is a state of mind which you may develop at will, after you have mastered the thirteen principles, because it is a state of mind which develops voluntarily, through application and use of these principles. Repetition of affirmation of orders to your subconscious mind is the only known method of voluntary development of the emotion of faith.

Note: Faith can be a result of life experience plus intuition plus knowledge plus properly applied intellectual ability. To develop faith concerning a particular area of your life, you can consciously focus on that area, and apply the newly discovered principles in addition to the ones described in this book. The New Science has now followed the purely theoretic New Thought, and innumerable scientific experiments have backed up the somehow vague presuppositions. Besides, better precision is achieved thanks to new discoveries in physics (Lynne McTaggart, "The Field").

Any impulse of thought which is repeatedly passed on to the subconscious mind is, finally, accepted and acted upon by the subconscious mind, which proceeds to translate that impulse into its physical equivalent, by the most practical procedure available. In connection with this, consider again the statement, ALL THOUGHTS WHICH HAVE BEEN EMOTIONALIZED, (given feeling) AND MIXED WITH FAITH, begin immediately to translate themselves into their physical equivalent or counterpart.

The emotions, or the "feeling" portion of thoughts, are the factors which give thoughts vitality, life, and action. The emotions of Faith, Love, and Sex, when mixed with any thought impulse, give it greater action than any of these emotions can do singly. Not only thought impulses which have been mixed with FAITH, but those which have been mixed with any of the positive emotions, or any of the negative emotions, may reach, and influence the subconscious mind.

From this statement, you will understand that the subconscious mind will translate into its physical equivalent, a thought impulse of a negative or destructive nature, just as readily as it will act upon thought impulses of a positive or constructive nature. This accounts for the strange phenomenon which so many millions of people experience, referred to as "misfortune," or "bad luck." There are millions of people who BELIEVE themselves "doomed" to poverty and failure, because of some strange force over which they BELIEVE they have no control. They are the creators of their own "misfortunes," because of this negative BELIEF, which is picked up by the subconscious mind, and translated into its physical equivalent.

This is an appropriate place at which to suggest again that you may benefit, by passing on to your subconscious mind, any DESIRE which you wish translated into its physical equivalent, in a state of expectancy or BELIEF that the transmutation will actually take place. Your BELIEF, or FAITH, is the element which determines the action of your subconscious mind.

Conduct yourself just as you would, if you were ALREADY IN POSSESSION OF THE MATERIAL THING WHICH YOU ARE DEMANDING, when you call upon your subconscious mind. The subconscious mind will transmute into its physical equivalent, by the most direct and practical media available, any order which is given to it in a state of BELIEF, or FAITH that the order will be carried out.

Note: many authors have described the procedure of successful pretending (or answered prayer), and some have given scientific explanations why it works (you can consult, for example, Neville Goddard "Prayer – The Art of Believing", as well as books on prayer and belief by Gregg Braden, Esther Hicks, or others).

The mind comes, finally, to take on the nature of the influences which dominate it. Encourage the positive emotions as dominating forces of your mind, and discourage — and eliminate negative emotions. A mind dominated by positive emotions, becomes a favorable abode for the state of mind known as faith. A mind so dominated may, at will, give the subconscious mind instructions, which it will accept and act upon immediately.

FAITH IS A STATE OF MIND WHICH MAY BE

INDUCED BY AUTO-SUGGESTION.

All down the ages, the religionists have admonished struggling humanity to "have faith" in this, that, and the other dogma or creed, but they have failed to tell people HOW to have faith. They have not stated that "faith is a state of mind, and that it may be induced by self-suggestion."

In language which any normal human being can understand, we will describe all that is known about the principle through which FAITH may be developed, where it does not already exist.

Have Faith in yourself; Faith in the Infinite.

Before we begin, you should be reminded again that: FAITH is the "eternal elixir" which gives life, power, and action to the impulse of thought!

The foregoing sentence is worth reading a second time, and a third, and a fourth. It is worth reading aloud! FAITH is the starting point of all accumulation of riches! FAITH is the basis of all "miracles," and all mysteries which cannot be analyzed by the rules of science! FAITH is the only known antidote for FAILURE! FAITH is the element, the "chemical" which, when mixed with prayer, gives one direct communication with Infinite Intelligence. FAITH is the element which transforms the ordinary vibration of thought, created by the finite mind of man, into the spiritual equivalent. FAITH is the only agency through which the cosmic force of Infinite Intelligence can be harnessed and used by man.

EVERY ONE OF THE FOREGOING STATEMENTS IS CAPABLE OF PROOF! The proof is simple and easily demonstrated. It is wrapped up in the principle of auto-suggestion.

Let us center our attention, therefore, upon the subject of self-suggestion, and find out what it is, and what it is capable of achieving.

It is a well known fact that one comes, finally, to BELIEVE whatever one repeats to one's self, whether the statement be true or false. If a man repeats a lie over and over (because he is willing to believe it), he will eventually accept the lie as truth. Moreover, he will BELIEVE it to be the truth.

Every man is what he is, because of the DOMINATING THOUGHTS which he permits to occupy his mind. Thoughts which a man deliberately places in his own mind, and encourages with sympathy, and with which he mixes any one or more of the emotions, constitute the motivating forces, which direct and control his every movement, act, and deed!

Comes, now, a very significant statement of truth:

THOUGHTS WHICH ARE MIXED WITH ANY OF THE FEELINGS OF EMOTIONS, CONSTITUTE A "MAGNETIC" FORCE WHICH ATTRACTS, FROM THE VIBRATIONS OF THE ETHER, OTHER SIMILAR, OR RELATED THOUGHTS.

A thought thus "magnetized" with emotion may be compared to a seed which, when planted in fertile soil, germinates, grows, and multiplies itself over and over again, until that which was originally one small seed, becomes countless millions of seeds of the SAME BRAND!

The ether is a great cosmic mass of eternal forces of vibration. It is made up of both destructive vibrations and constructive vibrations. It carries, at all times, vibrations of fear, poverty, disease, failure, misery; and vibrations of prosperity, health, success, and happiness, just as surely as it carries the sound of hundreds of orchestrations of music, and hundreds of human voices, all of which maintain their own individuality.

From the great storehouse of the ether, the human mind is constantly attracting vibrations which harmonize with that which DOMINATES the human mind. Any thought, idea, plan, or purpose which one holds in one's mind attracts, from the vibrations of the ether, a host of its relatives, adds these "relatives" to its own force, and grows until it becomes the dominating, MOTIVATING MASTER of the individual in whose mind it has been housed.

Now, let us go back to the starting point, and become informed as to how the original seed of an idea, plan, or purpose may be planted in the mind. The information is easily conveyed: any idea, plan, or purpose may be placed in the mind through repetition of thought. This is why you are asked to write out a statement of your major purpose, or Definite Chief Aim, commit it to memory, and repeat it, in audible words, day after day, until these vibrations of sound have reached your subconscious mind.

We are what we are, because of the vibrations of thought which we pick up and register, through the stimuli of our daily environment.

Resolve to throw off the influences of any unfortunate environment, and to build your own life to ORDER.

Taking inventory of mental assets and liabilities, you will discover that your greatest weakness is lack of self-confidence. This handicap can be surmounted, and timidity translated into courage, through the aid of the principle of autosuggestion. The application of this principle may be made through a simple arrangement of positive thought impulses stated in writing, memorized, and repeated, until they become a part of the working equipment of the subconscious faculty of your mind.

SELF-CONFIDENCE FORMULA

❑ First. I know that I have the ability to achieve the object of my Definite Purpose in life, therefore, I DEMAND of myself persistent, continuous action toward its attainment, and I here and now promise to render such action.

❑ Second. I realize the dominating thoughts of my mind will eventually reproduce themselves in outward, physical action, and gradually transform themselves into physical reality, therefore, I will concentrate my thoughts for thirty minutes daily, upon the task of thinking of the person I intend to become, thereby creating in my mind a clear mental picture of that person.

❑ Third. I know through the principle of auto-suggestion, any desire that I persistently hold in my mind will eventually seek expression through some practical means of attaining the object back of it, therefore, I will devote ten minutes daily to demanding of myself the development of SELF-CONFIDENCE.

❑ Fourth. I have clearly written down a description of my DEFINITE CHIEF AIM in life, and I will never stop trying, until I shall have developed sufficient self-confidence for its attainment.

❑ Fifth. I fully realize that no wealth or position can long endure, unless built upon truth and justice, therefore, I will engage in no transaction which does not benefit all whom it affects. *I will succeed by attracting to myself the forces I wish to use, and the cooperation of other people.* I will induce others to serve me, because of my willingness to serve others. I will eliminate hatred, envy, jealousy, selfishness, and cynicism, by developing love for all humanity, because I know that a negative attitude toward others can never bring me success. I will cause others to believe in me, because I will believe in them, and in myself.

I will sign my name to this formula, commit it to memory, and repeat it aloud once a day, with full FAITH that it will gradually influence my THOUGHTS and ACTIONS so that I will become a self-reliant, and successful person.

Back of this formula is a law of Nature which no man has yet been able to explain. It has baffled the scientists of all ages. The psychologists have named this law "auto-suggestion".

The subconscious mind, (the chemical laboratory in which all thought impulses are combined, and made ready for translation into physical reality), makes no distinction between constructive and destructive thought impulses. It works with the material we feed it, through our thought impulses. The subconscious mind will translate into reality a thought driven by FEAR just as readily as it will translate into reality a thought driven by COURAGE, or FAITH.

Just as electricity will turn the wheels of industry, and render useful service if used constructively; or snuff out life if wrongly used, so will the law of auto-suggestion lead you to peace and prosperity or down into the valley of misery, failure, and death, according to your degree of understanding and application of it.

If you fill your mind with FEAR, doubt and unbelief in your ability to connect with, and use the forces of Infinite Intelligence, the law of auto-suggestion will take this spirit of unbelief and use it as a pattern by which your subconscious mind will translate it into its physical equivalent.

Like the wind which carries one ship East, and another West, the law of auto-suggestion will lift you up or pull you down, according to the way you set your sails of THOUGHT.

Somewhere in your make-up (perhaps in the cells of your brain) there lies sleeping, the seed of achievement which, if aroused and put into action, would carry you to heights, such as you may never have hoped to attain. Just as a master musician may cause the most beautiful strains of music to pour forth from the strings of a violin, so may you arouse the genius lying asleep in your brain, and cause it to drive you upward to whatever goal you may wish to achieve.

Abraham Lincoln was a failure at everything he tried, until he was well past the age of forty. He was a Mr. Nobody from Nowhere, until a great experience came into his life, aroused the sleeping genius within his heart and brain, and gave the world one of its really great men. That "experience" was mixed with the emotions of sorrow and LOVE. It came to him through Anne Rutledge, the only woman whom he ever truly loved. It is a known fact that the emotion of LOVE is closely akin to the state of mind known as FAITH, and this for the reason that Love comes very near to translating one's thought impulses into their spiritual equivalent.

During his work of research, the author discovered, from the analysis of the life-work and achievements of hundreds of men of outstanding accomplishment, that there was the influence of a woman's love back of nearly EVERY ONE OF THEM. The emotion of love, in the human heart and brain, creates a favorable field of magnetic attraction, which causes an influx of the higher and finer vibrations which are afloat in the ether.

If you wish evidence of the power of FAITH, study the achievements of men and women who have employed it. At the head of the list comes the Nazarene. Christianity is the greatest single force which influences the minds of men. The basis of Christianity is FAITH, no matter how many people may have perverted, or misinterpreted the meaning of this great force, and no matter how many dogmas and creeds have been created in its name, which do not reflect its tenets.

The sum and substance of the teachings and the achievements of Christ, which may have been interpreted as "miracles," were nothing more nor less than FAITH. If there are any such phenomena as "miracles" they are produced only through the state of mind known as FAITH!

Some teachers of religion, and many who call themselves Christians, neither understand nor practice FAITH.

Let us consider the power of FAITH, as it is now being demonstrated, by a man who is well known to all of civilization, Mahatma Gandhi, of India. In this man the world has one of the most astounding examples known to civilization, of the possibilities of FAITH. Gandhi wields more potential power than any man living at this time, and this, despite the fact that he has none of the orthodox tools of power, such as money, battle ships, soldiers, and materials of warfare.

Gandhi has no money, he has no home, he does not own a suit of clothes, but HE DOES HAVE POWER. How does he come by that power? HE CREATED IT OUT OF HIS UNDERSTANDING OF THE PRINCIPLE OF FAITH, AND THROUGH HIS ABILITY TO TRANS- PLANT THAT FAITH INTO THE MINDS OF TWO HUNDRED MILLION PEOPLE.

Gandhi has accomplished, through the influence of FAITH, that which the strongest military power on earth could not, and never will accomplish through soldiers and military equipment. He has accomplished the astounding feat of INFLUENCING two hundred million minds to COALESCE AND MOVE IN UNISON, AS A SINGLE MIND.

What other force on earth, except FAITH could do as much? There will come a day when employees as well as employers will discover the possibilities of FAITH. That day is dawning.

Business is due for a reform, make no mistake about this! The methods of the past, based upon economic combinations of FORCE and FEAR, will be supplanted by the better principles of FAITH and cooperation. Men who labor will receive more than daily wages; they will receive dividends from the business, the same as those who supply the capital for business; but, first they must GIVE MORE TO THEIR EMPLOYERS, and stop this bickering and bargaining by force, at the expense of the public. They must earn the right to dividends!

Moreover, and this is the most important thing of all—THEY WILL BE LED BY LEADERS WHO WILL UNDERSTAND AND APPLY THE PRINCIPLES EMPLOYED BY MAHATMA GANDHI. Only in this way may leaders get from their followers the spirit of FULL cooperation which constitutes power in its highest and most enduring form.

This stupendous age in which we live, and from which we are just emerging, has taken the soul out of men. Its leaders have driven men as though they were pieces of cold machinery; they were forced to do so by the employees who have bargained, at the expense of all concerned, to get and not to give.

The watchword of the future will be HUMAN HAPPINESS AND CONTENTMENT, and when this state of mind shall have been attained, the production will take care of itself, more effectively than anything that has ever been accomplished where men did not, and could not mix FAITH and individual interest with their labor. Because of the need for faith and cooperation in operating business and industry, it will be both interesting and profitable to analyze an event which provides an excellent understanding of the method by which industrialists and business men accumulate great fortunes, by giving before they try to get.

RICHES begin in the form of THOUGHT! The amount is limited only by the person in whose mind the THOUGHT is put into motion. FAITH removes limitations! Remember this when you are ready to bargain with Life for whatever it is that you ask as your price for having passed this way.

THERE ARE NO LIMITATIONS TO THE MIND EXCEPT THOSE WE ACKNOWLEDGE

BOTH POVERTY AND RICHES ARE THE OFFSPRING OF THOUGHT

CHAPTER 4.
AUTO-SUGGESTION

THE MEDIUM FOR INFLUENCING THE SUBCONSCIOUS MIND

The Third Step toward Riches

AUTOSUGGESTION is the agency of control through which an individual may voluntarily feed his subconscious mind on thoughts of a creative nature, or, by neglect, permit thoughts of a destructive nature to find their way into this rich garden of the mind.

You were instructed, in the last of the six steps described in the chapter on Desire, to read ALOUD twice daily the WRITTEN statement of your DESIRE FOR MONEY, and to SEE AND FEEL yourself ALREADY in possession of the money! By following these instructions, you communicate the object of your DESIRE directly to your SUBCONSCIOUS mind in a spirit of absolute FAITH. Through repetition of this procedure, you voluntarily create thought habits which are favorable to your efforts to transmute desire into its monetary equivalent.

Go back to these six steps described in chapter two, and read them again, very carefully, before you proceed further. Then (when you come to it), read very carefully the four instructions for the organization of your "Master Mind" group, described in the chapter on Organized Planning. By comparing these two sets of instructions with that which has been stated on auto-suggestion, you, of course, will see that the instructions involve the application of the principle of auto-suggestion.

Remember, therefore, when reading aloud the statement of your desire (through which you are endeavoring to develop a "money consciousness"), that the mere reading of the words is of NO CONSEQUENCE—UNLESS you mix emotion, or feeling with your words. If you repeat a million times the famous Emil Coué formula,

"Day by day, in every way, I am getting better and better," without mixing emotion and FAITH with your words, you will experience no desirable results. Your subconscious mind recognizes and acts upon ONLY thoughts which have been well-mixed with emotion or feeling.

Note: Gregg Braden in his book "The Secrets of the Lost Mode of Prayer" makes a strong case for, that feeling is the prayer, and the way we feel about a matter ultimately defines the process and the outcomes. There is also a hypothesis, that no matter exists as such: all matter originates and exists only by virtue of a force that brings it to vibration, and this force is feeling.

This is a fact of such importance as to warrant repetition in practically every chapter, because the lack of understanding of this is the main reason the majority of people who try to apply the principle of auto-suggestion get no desirable results.

Plain, unemotional words do not influence the subconscious mind. You will get no appreciable results until you learn to reach your subconscious mind with thoughts, or spoken words which have been well emotionalized with BELIEF.

Wisdom and "cleverness" alone will not attract and retain money except in a few very rare instances, where the law of averages favors the attraction of money through these sources. The method of attracting money described here does not depend upon the law of averages. Moreover, the method plays no favorites. It will work for one person as effectively as it will for another.

Your ability to use the principle of auto-suggestion will depend, very largely, upon your capacity to CONCENTRATE upon a given DESIRE until that desire becomes a BURNING OBSESSION. When you begin to carry out the instructions in connection with the six steps described in the second chapter, it will be necessary for you to make use of the principle of CONCENTRATION.

Let us here offer suggestions for the effective use of concentration. When you begin to carry out the first of the six steps, which instructs you to "fix in your own mind the EXACT amount of money you desire," hold your thoughts on that amount of money by CONCENTRATION, or fixation of attention, with your eyes closed, until you can ACTUALLY SEE the physical appearance of the money. Do this at least once each day. As you go through these exercises, follow the instructions given in the chapter on FAITH, and see yourself actually IN POSSESSION OF THE MONEY!

Here is a most significant fact—the subconscious mind takes any orders given it in a spirit of absolute FAITH, and acts upon those orders, although the orders often have to be presented over and over again, through repetition, before they are interpreted by the subconscious mind. Following the preceding statement, consider the possibility of playing a perfectly legitimate "trick" on your subconscious mind, by making it believe, because you believe it, that you must have the amount of money you are visualizing, that this money is already awaiting your claim, that the subconscious mind MUST hand over to you practical plans for acquiring the money which is yours.

Hand over the thought suggested in the preceding paragraph to your IMAGINATION, and see what your imagination can, or will do, to create practical plans for the accumulation of money through transmutation of your desire.

DO NOT WAIT for a definite plan, through which you intend to exchange services or merchandise in return for the money you are visualizing, but begin at once to see yourself in possession of the money, DEMANDING and EXPECTING meanwhile, that your subconscious mind will hand over the plan, or plans you need. Be on the alert for these plans, and when they appear, put them into ACTION IMMEDIATELY.

When the plans appear, they will probably "flash" into your mind through the sixth sense, in the form of an "inspiration." This inspiration may be considered a direct "telegram," or message from Infinite Intelligence. Treat it with respect, and act upon it as soon as you receive it. Failure to do this will be FATAL to your success.

In the fourth of the six steps, you were instructed to "Create a definite plan for carrying out your desire, and begin at once to put this plan into action." You should follow this instruction in the manner described in the preceding paragraph. Do not trust to your "reason when creating your plan for accumulating money through the transmutation of desire. Your reason is faulty. Moreover, your reasoning faculty may be lazy, and, if you depend entirely upon it to serve you, it may disappoint you.

When visualizing the money you intend to accumulate, (with closed eyes), see yourself rendering the service, or delivering the merchandise you intend to give in return for this money. This is important!

SUMMARY OF INSTRUCTIONS

The fact that you are reading this book is an indication that you earnestly seek knowledge. It is also an indication that you are a student of this subject. If you are only a student, there is a chance that you may learn much that you did not know, but you will learn only by assuming an attitude of humility. If you choose to follow some of the instructions but neglect, or refuse to follow others-you will fail! To get satisfactory results, you must follow ALL instructions in a spirit of FAITH. The instructions given in connection with the six steps in the second chapter will now be summarized, and blended with the principles covered by this chapter, as follows:

☐ First. Go into some quiet spot (preferably in bed at night) where you will not be disturbed or interrupted, close your eyes, and repeat aloud, (so you may hear your own words) the written statement of the amount of money you intend to accumulate, the time limit for its accumulation, and a description of the service or merchandise you intend to give in return for the money. As you carry out these instructions, SEE YOURSELF ALREADY IN POSSESSION OF THE MONEY. For example :—Suppose that you intend to accumulate $50,000 by the first of January, five years hence, that you intend to give personal services in return for the money, in the Capacity of a salesman. Your written statement of your purpose should be similar to the following: "By the first day of January, 19.., I will have in my possession $50,000, which will come to me in various amounts from time to time during the interim. "In return for this money I will give the most efficient service of which I am capable, rendering the fullest possible quantity, and the best possible quality of service in the capacity of salesman of (describe the service or merchandise you intend to sell). "I believe that I will have this money in my possession. My faith is so strong that I can now see this money before my eyes. I can touch it with my hands. It is now awaiting transfer to me at the time, and in the proportion that I deliver the service I intend to render in return for it. I am awaiting a plan by which to accumulate this money, and I will follow that plan, when it is received."

❑ Second. Repeat this program night and morning until you can see, (in your imagination) the money you intend to accumulate.

❑ Third. Place a written copy of your statement where you can see it night and morning, and read it just before retiring, and upon arising until it has been memorized.

Remember, as you carry out these instructions, that you are applying the principle of auto-suggestion, for the purpose of giving orders to your subconscious mind. Remember, also, that your subconscious mind will act ONLY upon instructions which are emotionalized, and handed over to it with "feeling." FAITH is the strongest, and most productive of the emotions. Follow the instructions given in the chapter on FAITH.

These instructions may, at first, seem abstract. Do not let this disturb you. Follow the instructions, no matter how abstract or impractical they may, at first, appear to be. The time will soon come, if you do as you have been instructed, in spirit as well as in act, when a whole new universe of power will unfold to you.

Scepticism, in connection with ALL new ideas, is characteristic of all human beings. But if you follow the instructions outlined, your scepticism will soon be replaced by belief, and this, in turn, will soon become crystallized into ABSOLUTE FAITH. Then you will have arrived at the point where you may truly say, "I am the master of my fate, I am the captain of my soul!"

Many philosophers have made the statement, that man is the master of his own earthly destiny, but most of them have failed to say why he is the master. The reason that man may be the master of his own earthly status, and especially his financial status, is thoroughly explained in this chapter. Man may become the master of himself, and of his environment, because he has the POWER TO INFLUENCE HIS OWN SUBCONSCIOUS MIND, and through it, gain the cooperation of Infinite Intelligence.

You are now reading the chapter which represents the keystone to the arch of this philosophy. The instructions contained in this chapter must be understood and APPLIED WITH PERSISTENCE, if you succeed in transmuting desire into money.

The actual performance of transmuting DESIRE into money, involves the use of auto-suggestion as an agency by which one may reach, and influence, the subconscious mind. The other principles are simply tools with which to apply auto-suggestion. Keep this thought in mind, and you will, at all times, be conscious of the important part the principle of auto-suggestion is to play in your efforts to accumulate money through the methods described in this book.

Carry out these instructions as though you were a small child. Inject into your efforts something of the FAITH of a child. The author has been most careful, to see that no impractical instructions were included, because of his sincere desire to be helpful.

Note: In the absence of strong evidence, faith comes to those who apply any given set of principles in hope that they are true. Afterwards, faith starts to feed back to their adepts those very experiences that have been created in their subconscious minds through hope. Every mode and style of faith is possible. Start with this suggestion and create for yourself environments, connections, maybe even communities (or at least a mastermind group) that support your desired beliefs, and the reflection of these beliefs will soon be fed back to you as the experiences of your life. Choose only those you truly wish for. It makes no sense to choose someone else's goal, dream or wish – although your mind can accept other people's agendas, the result will never be to your taste.

CHAPTER 5
SPECIALIZED KNOWLEDGE

PERSONAL EXPERIENCES OR OBSERVATIONS

The Fourth Step toward Riches

General knowledge, no matter how great in quantity or variety it may be, is of but little use in the accumulation of money. The faculties of the great universities possess, in the aggregate, practically every form of general knowledge known to civilization. Most of the professors have but little or no money. They specialize on teaching knowledge, but they do not specialize on the organization, or the use of knowledge.

KNOWLEDGE will not attract money, unless it is organized, and intelligently directed, through practical PLANS OF ACTION, to the DEFINITE END of accumulation of money. Lack of under-standing of this fact has been the source of confusion to millions of people who falsely believe that "knowledge is power." It is nothing of the sort! Knowledge is only potential power. It becomes power only when, and if, it is organized into definite plans of action, and directed to a definite end.

This "missing link" in all systems of education known to civilization today, may be found in the failure of educational institutions to teach their students HOW TO ORGANIZE AND USE KNOWLEDGE AFTER THEY ACQUIRE IT.

That word "educate" is derived from the Latin word "educo," meaning to educe, to draw out, to DEVELOP FROM WITHIN.

An educated man is not, necessarily, one who has an abundance of general or specialized knowledge. An educated man is one who has so developed the faculties of his mind that he may acquire anything he wants, or its equivalent, without violating the rights of others.

Before you can be sure of your ability to transmute DESIRE into its monetary equivalent, you will require SPECIALIZED KNOWLEDGE of the service, merchandise, or profession which you intend to offer in return for fortune. Perhaps you may need much more specialized knowledge than you have the ability or the inclination to acquire, and if this should be true, you may bridge your weakness through the aid of your "Master Mind" group.

The accumulation of great fortunes calls for POWER, and power is acquired through highly organized and intelligently directed specialized knowledge, but that knowledge does not, necessarily, have to be in the possession of the man who ac-cumulates the fortune.

The preceding paragraph should give hope and encouragement to the man with ambition to accumulate a fortune, who has not possessed himself of the necessary "education" to supply such specialized knowledge as he may require. Men sometimes go through life suffering from "inferiority complexes," because they are not men of "education." The man who can organize and direct a "Master Mind" group of men who possess knowledge useful in the accumulation of money, is just as much a man of education as any man in the group. REMEMBER THIS, if you suffer from a feeling of inferiority, because your schooling has been limited.

SPECIALIZED KNOWLEDGE is among the most plentiful, and the cheapest forms of service which may be had! If you doubt this, consult the payroll of any university.

IT PAYS TO KNOW HOW TO PURCHASE KNOWLEDGE

First of all, decide the sort of specialized knowledge you require, and the purpose for which it is needed. To a large extent your major purpose in life, the goal toward which you are working, will help determine what knowledge you need. With this question settled, your next move requires that you have accurate information concerning dependable sources of knowledge.

As knowledge is acquired it must be organized and put into use, for a definite purpose, through practical plans. Knowledge has no value except that which can be gained from its application to-ward some worthy end. This is one reason why college degrees are not valued more highly. They represent nothing but miscellaneous knowledge.

Successful men, in all callings, never stop acquiring specialized knowledge related to their major purpose, business, or profession.

There is one weakness in people for which there is no remedy. It is the universal weakness of LACK OF AMBITION!

Persons, especially salaried people, who schedule their spare time, to provide for home study, seldom remain at the bottom very long. Their action opens the way for the upward climb, removes many obstacles from their path, and gains the friendly interest of those who have the power to put them in the way of OPPORTUNITY.

The home study method of training is especially suited to the needs of employed people who find, after leaving school, that they must acquire additional specialized knowledge, but cannot spare the time to go back to school.

When a merchant finds that a certain line of merchandise is not selling, he usually supplants it with another that is in demand. The person whose business is that of marketing personal services must also be an efficient merchant. If his services do not bring adequate returns in one occupation, he must change to another, where broader opportunities are available.

IT PAYS TO KNOW HOW TO PURCHASE KNOWLEDGE!

The person who stops studying merely because he has finished school is forever hopelessly doomed to mediocrity, no matter what may be his calling. The way of success is the way of continuous pursuit of knowledge.

Specialized knowledge, plus imagination, can be the ingredients that go into some unique and successful business. The beginning of such successful business is an IDEA!

"Why go to all this trouble?" do you ask? DOING A THING WELL NEVER IS TROUBLE!

I am also trying to emphasize another point, namely, that both success and failure are largely the results of HABIT.

Those searching for OPPORTUNITY will find valuable aid in the chapter on Organized Planning. Incidentally, an efficient merchandiser of personal services would find a growing demand for his services wherever there are people who seek better markets for their services. By applying the Master Mind principle, a few people with suitable talent, could form an alliance, and have a paying business very quickly. One would need to be a fair writer, with a flair for advertising and selling, some should provide the services, and one should be a first class business getter who would let the world know about the service. If one person possessed all these abilities, he might carry on the business alone, until it outgrew him.

If you have the IMAGINATION, and seek a more profitable outlet for your personal services, this suggestion may be the stimulus for which you have been searching. The IDEA is capable of yielding an income far greater than that of the "average" doctor, lawyer, or engineer whose education required several years in college. The idea is saleable to those seeking new positions, in practically all positions calling for managerial or executive ability, and those desiring re-arrangement of incomes in their present positions.

There is no fixed price for sound IDEAS!

Back of all IDEAS is specialized knowledge. Unfortunately, for those who do not find riches in abundance, specialized knowledge is more abundant and more easily acquired than IDEAS. Because of this very truth, there is a universal demand and an ever-increasing opportunity for the person capable of helping others to sell their personal services advantageously. Capability means IMAGINATION, the one quality needed to combine specialized knowledge with IDEAS, in the form of ORGANIZED PLANS designed to yield riches.

If you have IMAGINATION this chapter may present you with an idea sufficient to serve as the beginning of the riches you desire. Remember, the IDEA is the main thing. Specialized knowledge may be found just around the corner — any corner!

CHAPTER 6
IMAGINATION

THE WORKSHOP OF THE MIND

The Fifth Step toward Riches

The imagination is literally the workshop wherein are fashioned all plans created by man. The impulse, the DESIRE, is given shape, form, and ACTION through the aid of the imaginative faculty of the mind. It has been said that man can create anything which he can imagine. Of all the ages of civilization, this is the most favorable for the development of the imagination, because it is an age of rapid change. On every hand one may contact stimuli which develop the imagination.

MAN'S ONLY LIMITATION, within reason, LIES IN HIS DEVELOPMENT AND USE OF HIS IMAGINATION. He has not yet reached the apex of development in the use of his imaginative faculty. He has merely discovered that he has an imagination, and has commenced to use it in a very elementary way.

TWO FORMS OF IMAGINATION

SYNTHETIC IMAGINATION: Through this faculty, one may arrange old concepts, ideas, or plans into new combinations. This faculty creates nothing. It merely works with the material of experience, education, and observation with which it is fed. It is the faculty used most by the inventor, with the exception of the who draws upon the creative imagination, when he cannot solve his problem through synthetic imagination.

CREATIVE IMAGINATION: Through the faculty of creative imagination, the finite mind of man has direct communication with Infinite Intelligence. It is the faculty through which "hunches" and "inspirations" are received. It is by this faculty that all basic, or new ideas are handed over to man.

- It is through this faculty that thought vibrations from the minds of others are received. It is through this faculty that one individual may "tune in," or communicate with the subconscious minds of other men.
- The creative imagination works automatically, in the manner described in subsequent pages. This faculty functions ONLY when the conscious mind is vibrating at an exceedingly rapid rate, as for example, when the conscious mind is stimulated through the emotion of a strong desire.
- The creative imagination works automatically, in the manner described in subsequent pages. This faculty functions ONLY when the conscious mind is vibrating at an exceedingly rapid rate, as for example, when the conscious mind is stimulated through the emotion of a strong desire.
- The creative faculty becomes more alert, more receptive to vibrations from the sources mentioned, in proportion to its development through USE. This statement is significant! Ponder over it before passing on.
- The great leaders of business, industry, finance, and the great artists, musicians, poets, and writers became great, because they developed the faculty of creative imagination.

Both the synthetic and creative faculties of imagination become more alert with use, just as any muscle or organ of the body develops through use. Your imaginative faculty may have become weak through inaction. It can be revived and made alert through USE. This faculty does not die, though it may become quiescent through lack of use.

Keep in mind as you follow these principles that the entire story of how one may convert DESIRE into money cannot be told in one statement. The story will be complete, only when one has MASTERED, ASSIMILATED, and BEGUN TO MAKE USE of all the principles.

Center your attention, for the time being, on the development of the **synthetic imagination**, because this is the faculty which you will use more often in the process of converting desire into money. Transformation of the intangible impulse, of DESIRE, into the tangible reality, of MONEY, calls for the use of a plan, or plans. These plans must be formed with the aid of the imagination, and mainly, with the synthetic faculty.

Read the entire book through, then come back to this chapter, and begin at once to put your imagination to work on the building of a plan, or plans, for the transformation of your DESIRE into money. Detailed instructions for the building of plans have been given in almost every chapter. Carry out the instructions best suited to your needs, reduce your plan to writing, if you have not already done so. The moment you complete this, you will have DEF-INITELY given concrete form to the intangible DESIRE. Read the preceding sentence once more. Read it aloud, very slowly, and as you do so, remember that the moment you reduce the statement of your desire, and a plan for its realization, to writing, you have actually TAKEN THE FIRST of a series of steps, which will enable you to convert the thought into its physical counterpart.

The earth on which you live, you, yourself, and every other material thing are the result of evolutionary change, through which microscopic bits of matter have been organized and arranged in an orderly fashion. Moreover—and this statement is of stupendous importance—this earth, every one of the billions of individual cells of your body, and every atom of matter, began as an intangible form of energy.

DESIRE is thought impulse! Thought impulses are forms of energy. When you begin with the thought impulse, DESIRE, to accumulate money, you are drafting into your service the same "stuff" that Nature used in creating this earth, and every material form in the universe, including the body and brain in which the thought impulses function.

As far as science has been able to determine, the entire universe consists of but two elements – matter and energy. Through the combination of energy and matter, has been created everything perceptible to man, from the largest star which floats in the heavens, down to, and including man, himself.

You are now engaged in the task of trying to profit by Nature's method. You are (sincerely and earnestly, we hope), trying to adapt yourself to Nature's laws, by endeavoring to convert DESIRE into its physical or monetary equivalent.

YOU CAN DO IT! IT HAS BEEN DONE BEFORE!

Note: If the miracle of human formation is possible, the miracle of human transformation is possible as well.

You can build a fortune through the aid of laws which are immutable. But, first, you must become familiar with these laws, and learn to USE them. Through repetition, and by approaching the description of these principles from every conceivable angle, the author hopes to reveal to you the secret through which every great fortune has been accumulated. Strange and paradoxical as it may seem, the "secret" is NOT A SECRET. Nature, herself, advertises it in the earth on which we live, the stars, the planets suspended within our view, in the elements above and around us, in every blade of grass, and every form of life within our vision.

Nature advertises this "secret" in the terms of biology, in the conversion of a tiny cell, so small that it may be lost on the point of a pin, into the HUMAN BEING now reading this line. The conversion of desire into its physical equivalent is, certainly, no more miraculous!

Do not become discouraged if you do not fully comprehend all that has been stated. Unless you have long been a student of the mind, it is not to be expected that you will assimilate all that is in this chapter upon a first reading. **But you will, in time, make good progress.**

The principles which follow will open the way for understanding of imagination. Assimilate that which you understand, as you read this philosophy for the first time, then, when you reread and study it, you will discover that something has happened to clarify it, and give you a broader understanding of the whole.

Note: the author refers to a synchronicity principle, which makes things you need to make a good progress, suddenly appear on your way.

Above all, DO NOT STOP, nor hesitate in your study of these principles until you have read the book at least three times, for then, you will not want to stop.

SUCCESS REQUIRES NO EXPLANATIONS

FAILURE PERMITS NO ALIBIS

CHAPTER 7
ORGANIZED PLANNING

THE CRYSTALLIZATION OF DESIRE INTO ACTION

The Sixth Step toward Riches

❑ Ally yourself with a group of as many people as you may need for the creation, and carrying out of your plan, or plans for the accumulation of money—making use of the "Master Mind" principle described in a later chapter. (Compliance with this instruction is absolutely essential. Do not neglect it.)

❑ Before forming your "Master Mind" alliance, decide what advantages, and benefits, you may offer the individual members of your group, in return for their cooperation. No one will work indefinitely without some form of compensation. No intelligent person will either request or expect another to work without adequate compensation, although this may not always be in the form of money.

❑ Arrange to meet with the members of your "Master Mind" group at least twice a week, and more often if possible, until you have jointly perfected the necessary plan, or plans for the accumulation of money.

❑ Maintain PERFECT HARMONY between yourself and every member of your "Master Mind" group. If you fail to carry out this instruction to the letter, you may expect to meet with failure. The "Master Mind" principle cannot obtain where PERFECT HARMONY does not prevail.

You are engaged in an undertaking of major importance to you. To be sure of success, you must have plans which are faultless. You must also have the advantage of the experience, education, native ability and imagination of other minds. This is in harmony with the methods followed by every person who has accumulated a great fortune. No individual has sufficient experience, education, native ability, and knowledge to insure the accumulation of a great fortune, without the cooperation of other people. Every plan you adopt, in your endeavor to accumulate wealth, should be the joint creation of yourself and every other member of your "Master Mind" group. You may originate your own plans, either in whole or in part, but SEE THAT THOSE PLANS ARE CHECKED, AND APPROVED BY THE MEMBERS OF YOUR "MASTER MIND" ALLIANCE.

If the first plan which you adopt does not work successfully, replace it with a new plan, if this new plan fails to work, replace it, in turn with still another, and so on, until you find a plan which DOES WORK. Right here is the point at which the majority of men meet with failure, because of their lack of PERSISTENCE in creating new plans to take the place of those which fail.

The most intelligent man living cannot succeed in accumulating money—nor in any other undertaking—without plans which are practical and workable. Just keep this fact in mind, and remember when your plans fail, that temporary defeat is not permanent failure. It may only mean that your plans have not been sound. Build other plans. Start all over again. Temporary defeat should mean only one thing, the certain knowledge that there is something wrong with your plan.

Your achievement can be no greater than your PLANS are sound. That may seem to be an axiomatic statement, but it is true.

NO FOLLOWER OF THIS PHILOSOPHY CAN REASONABLY EXPECT TO ACCUMULATE A FORTUNE WITHOUT EXPERIENCING "TEMPORARY DEFEAT." When defeat comes, accept it as a signal that your plans are not sound, rebuild those plans, and set sail once more toward your coveted goal. If you give up before your goal has been reached, you are a "quitter."

A QUITTER NEVER WINS-AND—A WINNER NEVER QUITS. Lift this sentence out, write it on a piece of paper in letters an inch high, and place it where you will see it every night before you go to sleep, and every morning before you go to work.

When you begin to select members for your "Master Mind" group, endeavor to select those who do not take defeat seriously.

Some people foolishly believe that only MONEY can make money. This is not true! DESIRE, transmuted into its monetary equivalent, through the principles laid down here, is the agency through which money is "made." Money, of itself, is nothing but inert matter. It cannot move, think, or talk, but it can "hear" when a man who DESIRES it, calls it to come!

PLANNING THE SALE OF SERVICES

The remainder of this chapter has been given over to a description of ways and means of marketing personal services. The information here conveyed will be of practical help to any person having any form of personal services to market, but it will be of priceless benefit to those who aspire to leadership in their chosen occupations.

Intelligent planning is essential for success in any undertaking designed to accumulate riches. Here will be found detailed instructions to those who must begin the accumulation of riches by selling personal services.

It should be encouraging to know that practically all the great fortunes began in the form of compensation for personal services, or from the sale of IDEAS. What else, except ideas and personal services, would one not possessed of property have to give in return for riches?

Broadly speaking, there are two types of people in the world. One type is known as LEADERS, and the other as FOLLOWERS. Decide at the outset whether you intend to become a leader in your chosen calling, or remain a follower. The difference in compensation is vast. The follower cannot reasonably expect the compensation to which a leader is entitled, although many followers make the mistake of expecting such pay.

It is no disgrace to be a follower. On the other hand, it is no credit to remain a follower. Most great leaders began in the capacity of followers. They became great leaders because they were INTELLIGENT FOLLOWERS. With few exceptions, the man who cannot follow a leader intelligently, cannot become an efficient leader. The man who can follow a leader most efficiently, is usually the man who develops into leadership most rapidly. An intelligent follower has many advantages, among them the OPPORTUNITY TO ACQUIRE KNOWLEDGE FROM HIS LEADER.

THE MAJOR ATTRIBUTES OF LEADERSHIP

The following are important factors of leadership:

❑ UNWAVERING COURAGE based upon knowledge of self, and of one's occupation.

❑ SELF-CONTROL. The man who cannot control himself, can never control others.

❑ A KEEN SENSE OF JUSTICE. It takes a sense of fairness and justice to command and retain the respect of his followers.

❑ DEFINITENESS OF DECISION. . The man who wavers in his decisions, shows that he is not sure of himself. He cannot lead others successfully.

❑ DEFINITENESS OF PLANS. The successful leader must plan his work, and work his plan.

❑ THE HABIT OF DOING MORE THAN PAID FOR. One of the leader's traits is willingness to do more than he requires of his followers.

❑ A PLEASING PERSONALITY. No slovenly, careless person can become a successful leader. Leadership calls for respect.

❑ SYMPATHY AND UNDERSTANDING. The successful leader must be in sympathy with his followers. Moreover, he must understand them and their problems.

- MASTERY OF DETAIL. Successful leadership calls for mastery of details of the leader's position.
- WILLINGNESS TO ASSUME FULL RE-SPONSIBILITY. The successful leader must be willing to assume responsibility for the mistakes and the shortcomings of his followers. If he tries to shift this responsibility, he will not remain the leader. If one of his followers makes a mistake, and shows himself incompetent, the leader must consider that it is he who failed.
- COOPERATION. The successful leader must understand, and apply the principle of cooperative effort and be able to induce his followers to do the same. Leadership calls for POWER, and power calls for COOPERATION.

THE NEW WAY OF MARKETING SERVICES "JOBS" ARE NOW "PARTNERSHIPS"

Men and women who market their services to best advantage in the future, must recognize the stupendous change which has taken place in connection with the relationship between employer and employee.

In the future, the "Golden Rule," and not the "Rule of Gold" will be the dominating factor in the marketing of merchandise as well as personal services. The future relationship between employers and their employees will be more in the nature of a partnership consisting of: the employer, the employee, and the public they serve.

This new way of marketing personal services is called new for many reasons, first, both the employer and the employee of the future will be considered as fellow-employees whose business it will be to SERVE THE PUBLIC EFFICIENTLY. In times past, employers, and employees have bartered among themselves, driving the best bargains they could with one another, not considering that in the final analysis they were, in reality, BARGAINING AT THE EXPENSE OF THE THIRD PARTY, THE PUBLIC THEY SERVED.

Both employers and employees will recognize that they are NO LONGER PRIVILEGED TO DRIVE BARGAINS AT THE EXPENSE

OF THOSE WHOM THEY SERVE. The real employer of the future will be the public. This should be kept uppermost in mind by every person seeking to market personal services effectively.

"Courtesy" and "Service" are the watch-words of merchandising today, and apply to the person who is marketing personal services even more directly than to the employer whom he serves, because, in the final analysis, both the employer and his employee are EMPLOYED BY THE PUBLIC THEY SERVE. If they fail to serve well, they pay by the loss of their privilege of serving.

"The wages of sin is death!" Many have read this in the Bible, but few have discovered its meaning. Now the entire world has been listening BY FORCE, to a sermon which might well be called "WHATSOEVER A MAN SOWETH, THAT SHALL HE ALSO REAP."

Nothing as widespread and effective as the depression could possibly be "just a coincidence." Behind the depression was a CAUSE. Nothing ever happens without a CAUSE. In the main, the cause of the depression is traceable directly to the worldwide habit of trying to REAP without SOWING. This should not be mistaken to mean that the depression represents a crop which the world is being FORCED to reap without having SOWN. The trouble is that the world sowed the wrong sort of seed.

These illustrations are brought to the attention of those who have personal services to market, to show that we are where we are, and what we are, because of our own conduct! If there is a principle of cause and effect, which controls business, finance, and transportation, this same principle controls individuals and determines their economic status.

WHAT IS YOUR "QQS" RATING?

The causes of success in marketing services EFFECTIVELY and permanently, have been clearly described. Unless those causes are studied, analyzed, understood and APPLIED, no man can market his services effectively and permanently. Every person must be his own salesman of personal services. The QUALITY and the QUANTITY of service rendered, and the SPIRIT in which it is rendered, determine to a large extent, the price, and the duration of employment. To market Personal services effectively, (which means a permanent market, at a satisfactory price, under pleasant con-ditions), one must adopt and follow the "QQS" formula which means that QUALITY, plus QUANTITY, plus the proper SPIRIT of cooperation, equals perfect salesmanship of service. Remember the "QQS" formula, but do more-APPLY IT AS A HABIT!

Let us analyze the formula to make sure we understand exactly what it means.

1. QUALITY of service shall be construed to mean the performance of every detail, in connection with your position, in the most efficient manner possible, with the object of greater efficiency always in mind.

2. QUANTITY of service shall be understood to mean the HABIT of rendering all the service of which you are capable, at all times, with the purpose of increasing the amount of service rendered as greater skill is developed through practice and experience. Emphasis is again placed on the word HABIT.

3. SPIRIT of service shall be construed to mean the HABIT of agreeable, harmonious conduct which will induce cooperation from associates and fellow employees.

Adequacy of QUALITY and QUANTITY of service is not sufficient to maintain a permanent market for your services. The conduct, or the SPIRIT in which you deliver service, is a strong determining factor in connection with both the price you receive, and the duration of employment.

Andrew Carnegie stressed this point more than others in connection with his description of the factors which lead to success in the marketing of personal services. He emphasized again, and again, the necessity for HARMONIOUS CONDUCT. He stressed the fact that he would not retain any man, no matter how great a QUANTITY, or how efficient the QUALITY of his work, unless he worked in a spirit of HARMONY. Mr. Carnegie insisted upon men being AGREEABLE.

To prove that he placed a high value upon this quality, he permitted many men who conformed to his standards to become very wealthy. Those who did not conform, had to make room for others.

The importance of a pleasing personality has been stressed, because it is a factor which enables one to render service in the proper SPIRIT. If one has a personality which PLEASES, and renders service in a spirit of HARMONY, these assets often make up for deficiencies in both the QUALITY, and the QUANTITY of service one renders. Nothing, however, can be SUCCESSFULLY SUBSTITUTED FOR PLEASING CONDUCT.

THE CAPITAL VALUE OF YOUR SERVICES

The person whose income is derived entirely from the sale of personal services is no less a merchant than the man who sells commodities, and it might well be added, such a person is subject to EXACTLY THE SAME RULES of conduct as the merchant who sells merchandise.

This has been emphasized, because the majority of people who live by the sale of personal services make the mistake of considering themselves free from the rules of conduct, and the responsibilities attached to those who are engaged in marketing commodities.

The new way of marketing services has practically forced both employer and employee into partnership alliances, through which both take into consideration the rights of the third party, THE PUBLIC THEY SERVE.

The day of the "go-getter" has passed. He has been supplanted by the "go-giver." High-pressure methods in business finally blew the lid off. There will never be the need to put the lid back on, because, in the future, business will be conducted by methods that will require no pressure.

The actual capital value of your brains may be determined by the amount of income you can produce (by marketing your services). A fair estimate of the capital value of your services may be made by multiplying your annual income by sixteen and two-thirds, as it is reasonable to estimate that your annual income represents six percent of your capital value. Money rents for 6% per annum. Money is worth no more than brains. It is often worth much less.

Competent "brains," if effectively marketed, represent a much more desirable form of capital than that which is required to conduct a business dealing in commodities, because "brains" are a form of capital which cannot be permanently depreciated through depressions, nor can this form of capital be stolen or spent. Moreover, the money which is essential for the conduct of business is as worthless as a sand dune, until it has been mixed with efficient "brains."

THE THIRTY MAJOR CAUSES OF FAILURE

HOW MANY OF THESE ARE HOLDING YOU BACK?

Life's greatest tragedy consists of men and women who earnestly try, and fail! The tragedy lies in the overwhelmingly large majority of people who fail, as compared to the few who succeed.

I have had the privilege of analyzing several thousand men and women, 98% of whom were classed as "failures." There is something radically wrong with a civilization, and a system of education, which permit 98% of the people to go through life as failures. But I did not write this book for the purpose of moralizing on the rights and wrongs of the world; that would require a book a hundred times the size of this one.

My analysis work proved that there are thirty major reasons for failure, and thirteen major principles through which people accumulate fortunes. In this chapter, a description of the thirty major causes of failure will be given. As you go over the list, check yourself by it, point by point, for the purpose of discovering how many of these causes-of-failure stand between you and success.

❑ UNFAVORABLE HEREDITARY BACKGROUND. There is but little, if anything, which can be done for people who are born with a deficiency in brain power. This philosophy offers but one method of bridging this weakness — through the aid of the Master Mind. Observe with profit, however, that this is the ONLY one of the thirty causes of failure which may not be easily corrected by any individual.

❑ LACK OF A WELL-DEFINED PURPOSE IN LIFE. There is no hope of success for the person who does not have a central purpose, or definite goal at which to aim. Ninety-eight out of every hundred of those whom I have analyzed, had no such aim.

❑ LACK OF AMBITION TO AIM ABOVE MEDIOCRITY. We offer no hope for the person who is so indifferent as not to want to get ahead in life, and who is not willing to pay the price.

❑ INSUFFICIENT EDUCATION. This is a handicap which may be overcome with comparative ease. Experience has proven that the best-educated people are often those who are known as "self-made," or self-educated. It takes more than a college degree to make one a person of education. Any person who is educated is one who has learned to get whatever he wants in life without violating the rights of others. Education consists, not so much of knowledge, but of knowledge effectively and persistently APPLIED. Men are paid, not merely for what they know, but more particularly for WHAT THEY DO WITH THAT WHICH THEY KNOW.

❑ LACK OF SELF-DISCIPLINE. Discipline comes through self-control. This means that one must control all negative qualities. Before you can control conditions, you must first control yourself. Self-mastery is the hardest job you will ever tackle. If you do not conquer self, you will be conquered by self. You may see at one and the same time both your best friend and your greatest enemy, by stepping in front of a mirror.

- ☐ ILL HEALTH. No person may enjoy outstanding success without good health. Many of the causes of ill health are subject to mastery and control. These, in the main are: overeating of foods not conducive to health, wrong habits of thought, giving expression to negatives, wrong use of and over indulgence in sex, lack of proper physical exercise, an inadequate supply of fresh air, due to improper breathing.

- ☐ UNFAVORABLE ENVIRONMENTAL INFLUENCES DURING CHILDHOOD. "As the twig is bent, so shall the tree grow."

- ☐ PROCRASTINATION. This is one of the most common causes of failure. Procrastination stands within the shadow of every human being, waiting his opportunity to spoil one's chances of success. Most of us go through life as failures, because we are waiting for the "time to be right" to start doing something worthwhile. Do not wait. The time will never be "just right." Start where you stand, and work with whatever tools you may have at your command, and better tools will be found as you go along.

- ☐ LACK OF PERSISTENCE. Most of us are good "starters" but poor "finishers" of everything we begin. Moreover, people are prone to give up at the first signs of defeat. There is no substitute for PERSISTENCE. The person who makes PERSISTENCE his watch-word, discovers that "Old Man Failure" finally becomes tired, and makes his departure. Failure cannot cope with PERSISTENCE.

- ☐ NEGATIVE PERSONALITY. There is no hope of success for the person who repels people through a negative personality. Success comes through the application of POWER, and power is attained through the cooperative efforts of other people. A negative personality will not induce cooperation.

- ☐ LACK OF CONTROLLED SEXUAL URGE. Sex energy is the most powerful of all the stimuli which move people into ACTION. Because it is the most powerful of the emotions, it must be controlled, through transmutation, and converted into other channels.

- UNCONTROLLED DESIRE FOR "SOMETHING FOR NOTHING." The gambling instinct drives millions of people to failure.

- LACK OF A WELL DEFINED POWER OF DECISION. Men who succeed reach decisions promptly, and change them, if at all, very slowly. Men who fail, reach decisions, if at all, very slowly, and change them frequently, and quickly. Indecision and procrastination are twin brothers. Where one is found, the other may usually be found also. Kill off this pair before they completely "hog-tie" you to the treadmill of FAILURE.

- ONE OR MORE OF THE SIX BASIC FEARS. These fears have been analyzed for you in a later chapter. They must be mastered before you can market your services effectively.

- WRONG SELECTION OF A MATE IN MARRIAGE. This a most common cause of failure. The relationship of marriage brings people intimately into contact. Unless this re-lationship is harmonious, failure is likely to follow. Moreover, it will be a form of failure that is marked by misery and unhappiness, destroying all signs of AMBITION.

- OVER-CAUTION. The person who takes no chances, generally has to take whatever is left when others are through choosing. Over-caution is as bad as under-caution. Both are extremes to be guarded against. Life itself is filled with the element of chance.

- WRONG SELECTION OF ASSOCIATES IN BUSINESS. This is one of the most common causes of failure in business. In marketing personal services, one should use great care to select an employer who will be an inspiration, and who is, himself, intelligent and successful. We emulate those with whom we associate most closely. Pick an employer who is worth emulating.

- SUPERSTITION AND PREJUDICE. Superstition is a form of fear. It is also a sign of ignorance. Men who succeed keep open minds and are afraid of nothing.

- WRONG SELECTION OF A VOCATION. No man can succeed in a line of endeavor which he does not like. The most essential step in the marketing of personal services is that of selecting an occupation into which you can throw yourself wholeheartedly.

❑ LACK OF CONCENTRATION OF EFFORT. The "jack-of-all-trades" seldom is good at any. Concentrate all of your efforts on one DEFINITE CHIEF AIM.

❑ THE HABIT OF INDISCRIMINATE SPENDING. The spend-thrift cannot succeed, mainly because he stands eternally in FEAR OF POVERTY. Form the habit of systematic saving by putting aside a definite percentage of your income. Money in the bank gives one a very safe foundation of COURAGE when bar-gaining for the sale of personal services. Without money, one must take what one is offered, and be glad to get it.

❑ LACK OF ENTHUSIASM. Without enthusiasm one cannot be convincing. Moreover, enthusiasm is contagious, and the person who has it, under control, is generally welcome in any group of people.

❑ INTOLERANCE. The person with a "closed" mind on any subject seldom gets ahead. Intolerance means that one has stopped acquiring knowledge. The most damaging forms of intolerance are those connected with religious, racial, and political differences of opinion.

❑ INTEMPERANCE. The most damaging forms of intemperance are connected with eating, strong drink, and sexual activities. Overindulgence in any of these is fatal to success.

❑ INABILITY TO COOPERATE WITH OTHERS. More people lose their positions and their big opportunities in life, because of this fault, than for all other reasons combined. It is a fault which no well-informed business man, or leader will tolerate.

❑ POSSESSION OF POWER THAT WAS NOT ACQUIRED THROUGH SELF EFFORT. (Sons and daughters of wealthy men, and others who inherit money which they did not earn). Power in the hands of one who did not acquire it gradually, is often fatal to success. QUICK RICHES are more dangerous than poverty.

❑ INTENTIONAL DISHONESTY. There is no substitute for honesty. One may be temporarily dishonest by force of circumstances over which one has no control, without permanent damage. But, there is NO HOPE for the person who is dishonest by choice. Sooner or later, his deeds will catch up with him, and he will pay by loss of reputation, and perhaps even loss of liberty.

❑ EGOTISM AND VANITY. These qualities serve as red lights which warn others to keep away. THEY ARE FATAL TO SUCCESS.

❑ GUESSING INSTEAD OF THINKING. Most people are too indifferent or lazy to acquire FACTS with which to THINK ACCURATELY. They prefer to act on "opinions" created by guesswork or snap-judgments.

❑ LACK OF CAPITAL. This is a common cause of failure among those who start out in business for the first time, without sufficient reserve of capital to absorb the shock of their mistakes, and to carry them over until they have established a REPUTATION.

❑ Under this, name any particular cause of failure from which you have suffered that has not been included in the foregoing list.

_____

❑ _____

_____

❑ _____

_____

In these thirty major causes of failure is found a description of the tragedy of life, which obtains for practically every person who tries and fails. It will be helpful if you can induce someone who knows you well to go over this list with you, and help to analyze you by the thirty causes of failure. It may be beneficial if you try this alone. Most people cannot see themselves as others see them. You may be one who cannot.

The oldest of admonitions is "Man, know thyself!" If you market merchandise successfully, you must know the merchandise. The same is true in marketing personal services. You should know all of your weaknesses in order that you may either bridge them or eliminate them entirely. You should know your strength in order that you may call attention to it when selling your services. You can know yourself only through accurate analysis.

It is one thing to WANT money—everyone wants more—but it is something entirely different to be WORTH MORE! Many people mistake their WANTS for their JUST DUES. Your financial requirements or wants have nothing whatever to do with your WORTH. Your value is established entirely by your ability to render useful service or your capacity to induce others to render such service.

TAKE INVENTORY OF YOURSELF:

28 QUESTIONS YOU SHOULD ANSWER

Annual self-analysis is an essential in the effective marketing of personal services, as is annual inventory in merchandising. Moreover, the yearly analysis should disclose a DECREASE IN FAULTS, and an increase in VIRTUES. One goes ahead, stands still, or goes backward in life. One's object should be, of course, to go ahead. Annual self-analysis will disclose whether advancement has been, made, and if so, how much. It will also disclose any backward steps one may have made. The effective marketing of personal services requires one to move forward even if the progress is slow.

Your annual self-analysis should be made at the end of each year, so you can include in your New Year's Resolutions any improvements which the analysis indicates should be made. Take this inventory by asking yourself the following questions, and by checking your answers with the aid of someone who will not permit you to deceive yourself as to their accuracy.

☑ SELF-ANALYSIS QUESTIONNAIRE FOR PERSONAL INVENTORY

- Have I attained the goal which I established as my objective for this year? (You should work with a definite yearly objective to be attained as a part of your major life objective).
- Have I delivered service of the best possible QUALITY of which I was capable, or could I have improved any part of this service?
- Have I delivered service in the greatest possible QUANTITY of which I was capable?
- Has the spirit of my conduct been harmonious, and cooperative at all times?
- Have I permitted the habit of PROCRASTINATION to decrease my efficiency, and if so, to what extent?
- Have I improved my PERSONALITY, and if so, in what ways?
- Have I been PERSISTENT in following my plans through to completion?
- Have I reached DECISIONS PROMPTLY AND DEFINITELY on all occasions?
- Have I permitted any one or more of the six basic fears to decrease my efficiency?
- Have I been either "over-cautious," or "under-cautious?"
- Has my relationship with my associates in work been pleasant, or unpleasant? If it has been unpleasant, has the fault been partly, or wholly mine?
- Have I dissipated any of my energy through lack of CONCENTRATION of effort?
- Have I been open minded and tolerant in connection with all subjects?
- In what way have I improved my ability to render service?
- Have I been intemperate in any of my habits?
- Have I expressed, either openly or secretly, any form of EGOTISM?
- Has my conduct toward my associates been such that it has induced them to RESPECT me?
- Have my opinions and DECISIONS been based upon guesswork, or accuracy of analysis and THOUGHT?

- ❑ Have I followed the habit of budgeting my time, my expenses, and my income, and have I been conservative in these budgets?
- ❑ How much time have I devoted to UNPROFITABLE effort which I might have used to better advantage?
- ❑ How may I RE-BUDGET my time, and change my habits so I will be more efficient during the coming year?
- ❑ Have I been guilty of any conduct which was not approved by my conscience?
- ❑ In what ways have I rendered MORE SERVICE AND BETTER SERVICE than I was paid to render?
- ❑ Have I been unfair to anyone, and if so, in what way?
- ❑ If I had been the purchaser of my own services for the year, would I be satisfied with my purchase?
- ❑ Am I in the right vocation, and if not, why not?
- ❑ Has the purchaser of my services been satisfied with the service I have rendered, and if not, why not?
- ❑ What is my present rating on the fundamental principles of success? (Make this rating fairly, and frankly, and have it checked by someone who is courageous enough to do it accurately).

Complete assimilation and understanding of the information here conveyed will be helpful in marketing one's own services, and it will also help one to become more analytical and capable of judging people. The information will be priceless to personnel directors, employment managers, and other executives charged with the selection of employees, and the maintenance of efficient organizations.

CHAPTER 8
DECISION

THE MASTERY OF PROCRASTINATION

The Seventh Step toward Riches

PROCRASTINATION, the opposite of DECISION, is a common enemy which practically every man must conquer. You will have an opportunity to test your capacity to reach quick and definite DECISIONS when you finish reading this book, and are ready to begin putting into ACTION the principles which it describes.

People who had accumulated fortunes well beyond the million dollar mark, disclosed the fact that every one of them had the habit of REACHING DECISIONS PROMPTLY, and of changing these decisions SLOWLY, if, and when they were changed. People who fail to accumulate money, without exception, have the habit of reaching decisions, IF AT ALL, very slowly, and of changing these decisions quickly and often.

The majority of people who fail to accumulate money sufficient for their needs, are, generally, easily influenced by the "opinions" of others. They permit the newspapers and the "gossiping" neighbors to do their "thinking" for them. "Opinions are the cheapest commodities on earth. Everyone has a flock of opinions ready to be wished upon anyone who will accept them. If you are influenced by "opinions" when you reach DECISIONS, you will not succeed in any undertaking, much less in that of transmuting YOUR OWN DESIRE into money. If you are influenced by the opinions of others, you will have no DESIRE of your own.

Keep your own counsel, when you begin to put into practice the principles described here, by reaching your own decisions and following them. Take no one into your confidence, EXCEPT the members of your "Master Mind" group, and be very sure in your selection of this group, that you choose ONLY those who will be in COMPLETE SYMPATHY AND HARMONY WITH YOUR PURPOSE.

Close friends and relatives, while not meaning to do so, often handicap one through "opinions" and sometimes through ridicule, which is meant to be humorous. Thousands of men and women carry inferiority complexes with them all through life, because some well-meaning, but ignorant person destroyed their confidence through "opinions" or ridicule.

You have a brain and mind of your own. USE IT, and reach your own decisions. If you need facts or information from other people, to enable you to reach decisions, as you probably will in many instances; acquire these facts or secure the information you need quietly, without disclosing your purpose.

It is characteristic of people who have but a smattering or a veneer of knowledge to try to give the impression that they have much knowledge. Such people generally do TOO MUCH talking, and TOO LITTLE listening. Keep your eyes and ears wide open—and your mouth CLOSED, if you wish to acquire the habit of prompt DECISION. Those who talk too much do little else. If you talk more than you listen, you not only deprive yourself of many opportunities to accumulate useful knowledge, but you also disclose your PLANS and PURPOSES to people who will take great delight in defeating you, because they envy you.

Let one of your first decisions be to KEEP A CLOSED MOUTH AND OPEN EARS AND EYES.

"TELL THE WORLD WHAT YOU INTEND TO DO,

BUT FIRST SHOW IT."

CHAPTER 9
PERSISTENCE

THE SUSTAINED EFFORT NECESSARY TO INDUCE FAITH

The Eighth Step toward Riches

PERSISTENCE is an essential factor in the procedure of transmuting DESIRE into its monetary equivalent. The basis of persistence is the POWER OF WILL. Will-power and desire, when properly combined, make an irresistible pair. Men who accumulate great fortunes are generally known as cold-blooded, and sometimes ruthless. Often they are misunderstood. What they have is will-power, which they mix with persistence, and place back of their desires to insure the attainment of their objectives.

The majority of people are ready to throw their aims and purposes overboard, and give up at the first sign of opposition or misfortune. A few carry on DESPITE all opposition, until they attain their goal.

There may be no heroic connotation to the word "persistence," but the quality is to the character of man what carbon is to steel. The building of a fortune, generally, involves the application of the entire thirteen factors of this philosophy. These principles must be understood, they must be applied with PERSISTENCE by all who accumulate money.

Lack of persistence is one of the major causes of failure. Moreover, experience with thousands of people has proved that lack of persistence is a weakness common to the majority of men. It is a weakness which may be overcome by effort. The ease with which lack of persistence may be conquered will depend entirely upon the INTENSITY OF ONE'S DESIRE.

The starting point of all achievement is DESIRE. Keep this constantly in mind. Weak desires bring weak results, just as a small amount of fire makes a small amount of heat. If you find yourself lacking in persistence, this weakness may be remedied by building a stronger fire under your desires.

Continue to read through to the end, then go back to Chapter two, and start immediately to carry out the instructions given in connection with the six steps. The eagerness with which you follow these instructions will indicate clearly, how much, or how little you really DESIRE to accumulate money. If you find that you are indifferent, you may be sure that you have not yet acquired the "money consciousness" which you must possess, before you can be sure of accumulating a fortune.

Fortunes gravitate to men whose minds have been prepared to "attract" them, just as surely as water gravitates to the ocean. In this book may be found all the stimuli necessary to "attune" any normal mind to the vibrations which will attract the object of one's desires.

If you find you are weak in PERSISTENCE, center your attention upon the instructions contained in the chapter on "Power"; surround yourself with a "MASTER MIND" group, and through the cooperative efforts of the members of this group, you can develop persistence. You will find additional instructions for the development of persistence in the chapters on auto-suggestion, and the subconscious mind. Follow the instructions outlined in these chapters until your habit nature hands over to your subconscious mind, a clear picture of the object of your DESIRE. From that point on, you will not be handicapped by lack of persistence.

Your subconscious mind works continuously, while you are awake, and while you are asleep.

Spasmodic or occasional effort to apply the rules will be of no value to you. To get RESULTS, you must apply all of the rules until their application becomes a fixed habit with you. In no other way can you develop the necessary "money consciousness."

POVERTY is attracted to the one whose mind is favorable to it, as money is attracted to him whose mind has been deliberately prepared to attract it, and through the same laws. POVERTY CONSCIOUSNESS WILL VOLUNTARILY SEIZE THE MIND WHICH IS NOT OCCUPIED WITH THE MONEY CONSCIOUSNESS. A poverty consciousness develops without conscious application of habits favorable to it. The money consciousness must be created to order, unless one is born with such a consciousness.

Catch the full significance of the statements in the preceding paragraph, and you will understand the importance of PERSISTENCE in the accumulation of a fortune. Without PERSISTENCE, you will be defeated, even before you start. With PERSISTENCE you will win.

You may find it necessary to "snap" out of your mental inertia, through a similar procedure, moving slowly at first, then increasing your speed, until you gain complete control over your will. Be PERSISTENT no matter how slowly you may, at first, have to move. WITH PERSISTENCE WILL COME SUCCESS.

If you select your "Master Mind" group with care, you will have in it, at least one person who will aid you in the development of PERSISTENCE. Some men who have accumulated great fortunes, did so because of NECESSITY. They developed the habit of PERSISTENCE, because they were so closely driven by circumstances, that they had to become persistent.

THERE IS NO SUBSTITUTE FOR PERSISTENCE! It cannot be supplanted by any other quality! Remember this, and it will hearten you, in the beginning, when the going may seem difficult and slow.

Those who have cultivated the HABIT of persistence seem to enjoy insurance against failure. No matter how many times they are defeated, they finally arrive up toward the top of the ladder. Sometimes it appears that there is a hidden Guide whose duty is to test men through all sorts of discouraging experiences. Those who pick themselves up after defeat and keep on trying, arrive; and the world cries, "Bravo! I knew you could do it!" The hidden Guide lets no one enjoy great achievement without passing the PERSISTENCE TEST. Those who can't take it, simply do not make the grade.

Those who can "take it" are bountifully rewarded for their PERSISTENCE. They receive, as their compensation, whatever goal they are pursuing. That is not all! They receive something infinitely more important than material compensation—the knowledge that "EVERY FAILURE BRINGS WITH IT THE SEED OF AN EQUIVALENT ADVANTAGE."

There are exceptions to this rule; a few people know from experience the soundness of persistence. They are the ones who have not accepted defeat as being anything more than temporary. They are the ones whose DESIRES are so PERSISTENTLY APPLIED that defeat is finally changed into victory. We who stand on the side-lines of Life see the overwhelmingly large number who go down in defeat, never to rise again. We see the few who take the punishment of defeat as an urge to greater effort. These, fortunately, never learn to accept Life's reverse gear. But what we DO NOT SEE, what most of us never suspect of existing, is the silent but irresistible POWER which comes to the rescue of those who fight on in the face of discouragement. If we speak of this power at all we call it PERSISTENCE, and let it go at that. One thing we all know, if one does not possess PERSISTENCE, one does not achieve noteworthy success in any calling.

As these lines are being written, I look up from my work, and see before me, less than a block away, the great mysterious "Broadway," the "Graveyard of Dead Hopes," and the "Front Porch of Opportunity." From all over the world people have come to Broadway, seeking fame, fortune, power, love, or whatever it is that human beings call success. Once in a great while someone steps out from the long procession of seekers, and the world hears that another person has mastered Broadway. But Broadway is not easily nor quickly conquered. She acknowledges talent, recognizes genius, pays off in money, only after one has refused to QUIT.

Then we know who has discovered the secret of how to conquer Broadway. The secret is always inseparably attached to one word, PERSISTENCE!

Persistence is a state of mind, therefore it can be cultivated. Like all states of mind, persistence is based upon definite causes, among them these:

- ☑ DEFINITENESS OF PURPOSE. Knowing what one wants is the first and, perhaps, the most important step toward the development of persistence. A strong motive forces one to surmount many difficulties.
- ☑ DESIRE. It is comparatively easy to acquire and to maintain persistence in pursuing the object of intense desire.
- ☑ SELF-RELIANCE. Belief in one's ability to carry out a plan encourages one to follow the plan through with persistence. (Self-reliance can be developed through the principle described in the chapter on auto-suggestion).
- ☑ DEFINITENESS OF PLANS. Organized plans, even though they may be weak and entirely impractical, encourage persistence.
- ☑ ACCURATE KNOWLEDGE. Knowing that one's plans are sound, based upon experience or observation, encourages persistence; "guessing" instead of "knowing" destroys persistence.
- ☑ CO-OPERATION. Sympathy, understanding, and harmonious cooperation with others tend to develop persistence.
- ☑ WILL-POWER. The habit of concentrating one's thoughts upon the building of plans for the attainment of a definite purpose, leads to persistence.
- ☑ HABIT. Persistence is the direct result of habit. The mind absorbs and becomes a part of the daily experiences upon which it feeds. Fear, the worst of all enemies, can be effectively cured by forced repetition of acts of courage. Everyone who has seen active service in war knows this.

Before leaving the subject of PERSISTENCE, take inventory of yourself, and determine in what particular, if any, you are lacking in this essential quality. Measure yourself courageously, point by point, and see how many of the eight factors of persistence you lack. The analysis may lead to discoveries that will give you a new grip on yourself.

SYMPTOMS OF LACK OF PERSISTENCE

Here you will find the real enemies which stand between you and noteworthy achievement. Here you will find not only the "symptoms" indicating weakness of PERSISTENCE, but also the deeply seated subconscious causes of this weakness. Study the list carefully, and face yourself squarely IF YOU REALLY WISH TO KNOW WHO YOU ARE, AND WHAT YOU ARE CAPABLE OF DOING. These are the weaknesses which must be mastered by all who accumulate riches.

- ❑ Failure to recognize and to clearly define exactly what one wants.
- ❑ Procrastination, with or without cause. (Usually backed up with a formidable array of alibis and excuses).
- ❑ Lack of interest in acquiring specialized knowledge.
- ❑ Indecision, the habit of "passing the buck" on all occasions, instead of facing issues squarely. (Also backed by alibis).
- ❑ The habit of relying upon alibis instead of creating definite plans for the solution of problems.
- ❑ Self-satisfaction. There is but little remedy for this affliction, and no hope for those who suffer from it.
- ❑ Indifference, usually reflected in one's readiness to compromise on all occasions, rather than meet opposition and fight it.
- ❑ The habit of blaming others for one's mistakes, and accepting unfavorable circumstances as being unavoidable.
- ❑ WEAKNESS OF DESIRE, due to neglect in the choice of MOTIVES that impel action.

- ❑ Willingness, even eagerness, to quit at the first sign of defeat. (Based upon one or more of the 6 basic fears).
- ❑ Lack of ORGANIZED PLANS, placed in writing where they may be analyzed.
- ❑ The habit of neglecting to move on ideas, or to grasp opportunity when it presents itself.
- ❑ WISHING instead of WILLING.
- ❑ The habit of compromising with POVERTY instead of aiming at riches. General absence of ambition to be, to do, and to own.
- ❑ Searching for all the short-cuts to riches, trying to GET without GIVING a fair equivalent, usually reflected in the habit of gambling, endeavoring to drive "sharp" bargains.
- ❑ FEAR OF CRITICISM, failure to create plans and to put them into action, because of what other people will think, do, or say. This enemy belongs at the head of the list, because it generally exists in one's subconscious mind, where its presence is not recognized. (See the Six Basic Fears in a later chapter).

Let us examine some of the symptoms of the Fear of Criticism. The majority of people permit relatives, friends, and the public at large to so influence them that they cannot live their own lives, because they fear criticism. Huge numbers of people make mistakes in marriage, stand by the bargain, and go through life miserable and unhappy, because they fear criticism which may follow if they correct the mistake. (Anyone who has submitted to this form of fear knows the irreparable damage it does, by destroying ambition, self-reliance, and the desire to achieve).

Countless numbers of men and women, both young and old, permit relatives to wreck their lives in the name of DUTY, because they fear criticism. (Duty does not require any person to submit to the destruction of his personal ambitions and the right to live his own life in his own way).

People refuse to take chances in business, because they fear the criticism which may follow if they fail. **The fear of criticism, in such cases is stronger than the DESIRE for success.**

Too many people refuse to set high goals for themselves, or even neglect selecting a career, because they fear the criticism of relatives and "friends" who may say "Don't aim so high, people will think you are crazy".

MOST IDEAS ARE STILL-BORN, AND NEED THE BREATH OF LIFE INJECTED INTO THEM THROUGH DEFINITE PLANS OF IMMEDIATE ACTION. The time to nurse an idea is at the time of its birth. Every minute it lives, gives it a better chance of surviving. The FEAR OF CRITICISM is at the bottom of the destruction of most ideas which never reach the PLANNING and ACTION stage.

Many people believe that material success is the result of favorable "breaks." There is an element of ground for the belief, but those depending entirely upon luck, are nearly always disappointed, because they overlook another important factor which must be present before one can be sure of success. It is the knowledge with which favorable "breaks" can be made to order.

The only "break" anyone can afford to rely upon is a self-made "break." These come through the application of PERSISTENCE. The starting point is DEFINITENESS OF PURPOSE.

Examine the first hundred people you meet, ask them what they want most in life, and ninety eight of them will not be able to tell you. If you press them for an answer, some will say—SECURITY, many will say—MONEY, a few will say—HAPPINESS, others will say—FAME AND POWER, and still others will say—SOCIAL RECOGNITION, EASE IN LIVING, ABILITY TO SING, DANCE, or WRITE, but none of them will be able to define these terms, or give the slightest indication of a PLAN by which they hope to attain these vaguely expressed wishes. Riches do not respond to wishes. They respond only to definite plans, backed by definite desires, through constant PERSISTENCE.

HOW TO DEVELOP PERSISTENCE

There are four simple steps which lead to the habit of PERSISTENCE. They call for no great amount of intelligence, no particular amount of education, and but little time or effort. The necessary steps are:

- ❑ A DEFINITE PURPOSE BACKED BY BURNING DESIRE FOR ITS FULFILLMENT.
- ❑ A DEFINITE PLAN, EXPRESSED IN CONTINUOUS ACTION.
- ❑ A MIND CLOSED TIGHTLY AGAINST ALL NEGATIVE AND DISCOURAGING INFLUENCES, including negative suggestions of relatives, friends and acquaintances.
- ❑ A FRIENDLY ALLIANCE WITH ONE OR MORE PERSONS WHO WILL ENCOURAGE ONE TO FOLLOW THROUGH WITH BOTH PLAN AND PURPOSE.

These four steps are essential for success in all walks of life. The entire purpose of the thirteen principles of this philosophy is to enable one to take these four steps as a matter of habit.

These are the steps by which one may control one's economic destiny. They are the steps that lead to freedom and independence of thought. They are the steps that lead to riches, in small or great quantities. They lead the way to power, fame, and worldly recognition. They are the four steps which guarantee favorable "breaks." They are the steps that convert dreams into physical realities. They lead, also, to the mastery of FEAR, DISCOURAGEMENT, INDIFFERENCE.

There is a magnificent reward for all who learn to take these four steps. It is the privilege of writing one's own ticket, and of making Life yield whatever price is asked.

Note: The whole philosophy of success created by Napoleon Hill is about attaining that which we value highest in life. Here are the quotes following a

"Blessed is the man who has come to know that our muted thoughts are our sweetest thoughts. Blessed is the man who, from the blackest depths, can see the luminous figure of LOVE, and seeing, sing; and singing, say: 'Sweeter far than uttered lays are the thoughts I have of you.'"In these words would we pay tribute to the two people who, more than all others of modern times, have been the victims of criticism and the recipients of abuse, because they found Life's greatest treasure, and claimed it. Most of the world will applaud King Edward and Wallis Simpson, because of their PERSISTENCE in searching until they found life's greatest reward. ALL OF US CAN PROFIT by following their example in our own search for that which we demand of life.

What mystical power gives to men of PERSISTENCE the capacity to master difficulties? Does the quality of PERSISTENCE set up in one's mind some form of spiritual, mental or chemical activity which gives one access to supernatural forces? Does Infinite Intelligence throw itself on the side of the person who still fights on, after the battle has been lost, with the whole world on the opposing side?

As one makes an impartial study of the prophets, philosophers, "miracle" men, and religious leaders of the past, one is drawn to the inevitable conclusion that PERSISTENCE, concentration of effort, and DEFINITENESS OF PURPOSE, were the major sources of their achievements.

CHAPTER 10
POWER OF THE MASTER MIND

THE DRIVING FORCE

The Ninth Step toward Riches

POWER is essential for success in the accumulation of money. PLANS are inert and useless, without sufficient POWER to translate them into ACTION. This chapter will describe the method by which an individual may attain and apply POWER. POWER may be defined as "organized and intelligently directed KNOWLEDGE." Power, as the term is here used, refers to ORGANIZED effort, sufficient to enable an individual to transmute DESIRE into its monetary equivalent. ORGANIZED effort is produced through the coordination of effort of two or more people, who work toward a DEFINITE end, in a spirit of harmony. POWER IS REQUIRED FOR THE ACCUMULATION OF MONEY! POWER IS NECESSARY FOR THE RETENTION OF MONEY AFTER IT HAS BEEN ACCUMULATED!

If power is "organized knowledge," let us examine the sources of knowledge:

☑ INFINITE INTELLIGENCE. This source of knowledge may be contacted through the procedure described in another chapter ("The Sixth Sense"), with the aid of Creative Imagination.

☑ ACCUMULATED EXPERIENCE. The accumulated experience of man, (or that portion of it which has been organized and recorded), may be found in any well-equipped public library. An important part of this accumulated experience is taught in public schools and colleges, where it has been classified and organized.

☑ EXPERIMENT AND RESEARCH. In the field of science, and in practically every other walk of life, men are gathering, classifying, and organizing new facts daily. This is the source to which one must turn when knowledge is not available through "accumulated experience." Here, too, the Creative Imagination must often be used.

☑ *Note: It can be useful to collect and organize knowledge in relation to a particular aim. It can be necessary to create your own source library, which is accessible at any time and organized by some principle that gives meaning to you, especially while you are working on conceptualizing your idea.*

Knowledge may be acquired from any of the foregoing sources. It may be converted into POWER by organizing it into definite PLANS and by expressing those plans in terms of ACTION.

Examination of the three major sources of knowledge will readily disclose the difficulty an individual would have, if he depended upon his efforts alone, in assembling knowledge and expressing it through definite plans in terms of ACTION. If his plans are comprehensive, and if they contemplate large proportions, he must, generally, induce others to cooperate with him, before he can inject into them the necessary element of POWER.

GAINING POWER THROUGH THE "MASTER MIND"

The "Master Mind" may be defined as: "Coordination of knowledge and effort, in a spirit of harmony, between two or more people, for the attainment of a definite purpose." No individual may have great power without availing himself of the "Master Mind." In a preceding chapter, instructions were given for the creation of PLANS for the purpose of translating DESIRE into its physical equivalent. If you carry out these instructions with PERSISTENCE and intelligence, and use discrimination in the selection of your "Master Mind" group, your objective will have been half-way reached, even before you begin to recognize it.

So you may better understand the "intangible" potentialities of power available to you, through a properly chosen "Master Mind" group, we will here explain the two characteristics of the Master Mind principle, one of which is economic in nature, and the other psychic. The economic feature is obvious. Economic advantages may be created by any person who surrounds himself with the advice, counsel, and personal cooperation of a group of men who are willing to lend him wholehearted aid, in a spirit of PERFECT HARMONY. This form of cooperative alliance has been the basis of nearly every great fortune. Your understanding of this great truth may definitely determine your financial status.

The psychic phase of the Master Mind principle is much more abstract, much more difficult to comprehend, because it has reference to the spiritual forces with which the human race, as a whole, is not well acquainted. You may catch a significant sug-gestion from this statement: "No two minds ever come together without, thereby, creating a third, invisible, intangible force which may be likened to a third mind."

Keep in mind the fact that there are only two known elements in the whole universe, energy and matter. It is a well known fact that matter may be broken down into units of molecules, atoms, and electrons. There are units of matter which may be isolated, separated, and analyzed. Likewise, there are units of energy. The human mind is a form of energy, a part of it being spiritual in nature. When the minds of two people are coordinated in a SPIRIT OF HARMONY, the spiritual units of energy of each mind form an affinity, which constitutes the "psychic" phase of the Master Mind.

Any man who has accumulated a great fortune, and many of those who have accumulated modest fortunes, and you will find that they have either consciously, or unconsciously employed the "Master Mind" principle. GREAT POWER CAN BE ACCUMULATED THROUGH NO OTHER PRINCIPLE!

ENERGY is Nature's universal set of building blocks, out of which she constructs every material thing in the universe, including man, and every form of animal and vegetable life. Through a process which only Nature completely understands, she translates energy into matter. Nature's building blocks are available to man, in the energy involved in THINKING! Man's brain may be compared to an electric battery. It absorbs energy from the ether, which permeates every atom of matter, and fills the entire universe. A group of brains coordinated (or connected) in a spirit of harmony, will provide more thought-energy than a single brain, just as a group of electric batteries will provide more energy than a single battery.

Through this metaphor it becomes immediately obvious that the Master Mind principle holds the secret of the POWER wielded by men who surround themselves with other men of brains.

There follows, now, another statement which will lead still nearer to an understanding of the psychic phase of the Master Mind principle: When a group of individual brains are coordinated and function in Harmony, the increased energy created through that alliance, becomes available to every individual brain in the group.

We have already mentioned Mahatma Gandhi. Let us study the method by which he attained his stupendous POWER. It may be explained in a few words. He came by POWER through inducing over two hundred million people to coordinate, with mind and body, in a spirit of HARMONY, for a DEFINITE PURPOSE. In brief, Gandhi has accomplished a MIRACLE, for it is a miracle when two hundred million people can be induced—not forced—to cooperate in a spirit of HARMONY, for a limitless time. If you doubt that this is a miracle, try to induce ANY TWO PEOPLE to cooperate in a spirit of harmony for any length of time. Every man who manages a business knows what a difficult matter it is to get employees to work together in a spirit even remotely resembling HARMONY.

The list of the chief sources from which POWER may be attained is, as you have seen, headed by INFINITE INTELLIGENCE. When two or more people coordinate in a spirit of HARMONY, and work toward a definite objective, they place themselves in position, through that alliance, to absorb power directly from the great universal storehouse of Infinite Intelligence. This is the greatest of all sources of POWER. It is the source to which the genius turns. It is the source to which every great leader turns, (whether he may be conscious of the fact or not).

The other two major sources from which the knowledge, necessary for the accumulation of POWER, may be obtained are no more reliable than the five senses of man. The senses are not always reliable. Infinite Intelligence DOES NOT ERR.

*Note: It takes HEART to know the truth and know the way – beyond any doubt, **your particular truth and your particular way**.*

Read, THINK, and meditate as you read. Soon, the entire subject will unfold, and you will see it in perspective. You are now seeing the detail of the individual chapters.

When money comes in quantities known as "the big money," it flows to the one who accumulates it, as easily as water flows down hill. There exists a great unseen stream of POWER, which may be compared to a river; except that one side flows in one direction, carrying all who get into that side of the stream, onward and upward to WEALTH—and the other side flows in the opposite direction, carrying all who are unfortunate enough to get into it (and not able to extricate themselves from it), downward to misery and POVERTY.

Every man who has accumulated a great fortune, has recognized the existence of this stream of life. It consists of one's THINKING PROCESS. The positive emotions of thought form the side of the stream which carries one to fortune. The negative emotions form the side which carries one down to poverty.

If you are in the side of the stream of POWER which leads to poverty, this may serve as an oar, by which you may propel yourself over into the other side of the stream. It can serve you ONLY through application and use. Merely reading, and passing judgment on it, either one way or another, will in no way benefit you.

Some people undergo the experience of alternating between the positive and negative sides of the stream, being at times on the positive side, and at times on the negative side. They are struggling, some of them in desperation and fear, to get back to the positive side of the stream.

Poverty and riches often change places. Poverty may, and generally does, voluntarily take the place of riches. When riches take the place of poverty, the change is usually brought about through well conceived and carefully executed PLANS. Poverty needs no plan. It needs no one to aid it, because it is bold and ruthless. Riches are shy and timid. They have to be "attracted."

CHAPTER 11
THE MYSTERY OF SEX TRANSMUTATION

The Tenth Step toward Riches

The meaning of the word "transmute" is, in simple language, "the changing, or transferring of one element, or form of energy, into another." The emotion of sex brings into being a state of mind. Because of ignorance on the subject, this state of mind is generally associated with the physical, and because of improper influences, to which most people have been subjected, in acquiring knowledge of sex, things essentially physical have highly biased the mind. The emotion of sex has back of it the possibility of three constructive potentialities, they are:

1. The perpetuation of mankind.

2. The maintenance of health, (as a therapeutic agency, it has no equal).

3. The transformation of mediocrity into genius through transmutation.

Sex transmutation is simple and easily explained. It means the switching of the mind from thoughts of physical expression, to thoughts of some other nature.

Sex desire is the most powerful of human desires. When driven by this desire, men develop keenness of imagination, courage, will-power, persistence, and creative ability unknown to them at other times. So strong and impelling is the desire for sexual contact that men freely run the risk of life and reputation to indulge it. When harnessed, and redirected along other lines, this motivating force maintains all of its attributes of keenness of imagination, courage, etc., which may be used as powerful creative forces in literature, art, or in any other profession or calling, including, of course, the accumulation of riches.

The transmutation of sex energy calls for the exercise of will-power, to be sure, but the reward is worth the effort. The desire for sexual expression is inborn and natural. The desire cannot, and should not be submerged or eliminated. But it should be given an outlet through forms of expression which enrich the body, mind, and spirit of man. If not given this form of outlet, through transmutation, it will seek outlets through purely physical channels.

Note: I would like to draw the reader's attention to the fact that there exists a substitute for the will-power, and it is a healthy personality plus "a little bit of luck", as Doolittle sings in the movie version of Bernard Shaw's Pygmalion, "My Fair Lady".

A river may be dammed, and its water controlled for a time, but eventually, it will force an outlet. The same is true of the emotion of sex. It may be submerged and controlled for a time, but its very nature causes it to be ever seeking means of expression. If it is not transmuted into some creative effort it will find a less worthy outlet.

Fortunate, indeed, is the person who has discovered how to give sex emotion an outlet through some form of creative effort, for he has, by that discovery, lifted himself to the status of a genius.

The emotion of sex is an "irresistible force," against which there can be no such opposition as an "immovable body." When driven by this emotion, men become gifted with a super power for action. Understand this truth, and you will catch the significance of the statement that sex transmutation will lift one to the status of a genius. The emotion of sex contains the secret of creative ability.

THE TEN MIND STIMULI

1. The desire for sex expression

2. Love

3. A burning desire for fame, power, or financial gain

4. Music

5. Friendship between either those of the same sex, or those of the opposite sex.

6. A Master Mind alliance based upon the harmony of two or more people who ally themselves for spiritual or temporal advancement.

7. Mutual suffering, such as that experienced by people who are persecuted.

8. Auto-suggestion

9. Fear

10. Narcotics and alcohol.

The desire for sex expression comes at the head of the list of stimuli, which most effectively "stepup" the vibrations of the mind and start the "wheels" of physical action. Eight of these stimuli are natural and constructive. Two are destructive. The list is here presented for the purpose of enabling you to make a comparative study of the major sources of mind stimulation. From this study, it will be readily seen that the emotion of sex is, by great odds, the most intense and powerful of all mind stimuli. This comparison is necessary as a foundation for proof of the statement that transmutation of sex energy may lift one to the status of a genius. Let us find out what constitutes a genius.

A better definition of a genius is, "a man who has discovered how to increase the vibrations of thought to the point where he can freely communicate with sources of knowledge not available through the ordinary rate of vibration of thought."

The person who thinks will want to ask some questions concerning this definition of genius. The first question will be, "How may one communicate with sources of knowledge which are not available through the ORDINARY rate of vibration of thought?" The next question will be, "Are there known sources of knowledge which are available only to genii, and if so, WHAT ARE THESE SOURCES, and exactly how may they be reached?"

"GENIUS" IS DEVELOPED THROUGH THE SIXTH SENSE

The reality of a "sixth sense" has been fairly well established. This sixth sense is "Creative Imagination." The faculty of creative imagination is one which the majority of people never use during an entire lifetime, and if used at all, it usually happens by mere accident. A relatively small number of people use, WITH DELIBERATION AND PURPOSE AFORETHOUGHT, the faculty of creative imagination. Those who use this faculty voluntarily, and with understanding of its functions, are GENII.

The human mind responds to stimulation. Among the greatest, and most powerful of these stimuli is the urge of sex. When harnessed and transmuted, this driving force is capable of lifting men into that higher sphere of thought which enables them to master the sources of worry and petty annoyance which beset their pathway on the lower plane. Unfortunately, only the genii have made the discovery. Others have accepted the experience of sex urge, without discovering one of its major potentialities—a fact which accounts for the great number of "others" as compared to the limited number of genii. Although, the mere possession of sex energy is not sufficient to produce a genius. The energy must be transmuted from desire for physical contact, into some other form of desire and action, before it will lift one to the status of a genius. The desire for sexual expression is by far the strongest and most impelling of all the human emotions, and for this very reason this desire, when harnessed and transmuted into action, other than that of physical expression, may raise one to the status of a genius.

The faculty of creative imagination is the direct link between the finite mind of man and Infinite Intelligence. All so-called revelations, referred to in the realm of religion, and all discoveries of basic or new principles in the field of invention, take place through the faculty of creative imagination. When ideas or concepts flash into one's mind, through what is popularly called a "hunch," they come from one or more of the following sources:

1. Infinite Intelligence

2. One's subconscious mind, wherein is stored every sense impression and thought impulse which ever reached the brain through any of the five senses

3. From the mind of some other person who has just released the thought, or picture of the idea or concept, through conscious thought

4. From the other person's subconscious storehouse.

The creative imagination functions best when the mind is vibrating (due to some form of mind stimulation) at an exceedingly high rate. That is, when the mind is functioning at a rate of vibration higher than that of ordinary, normal thought.

When brain action has been stimulated, through one or more of the ten mind stimulants, it has the effect of lifting the individual far above the horizon of ordinary thought, and permits him to envision distance, scope, and quality of THOUGHTS not available on the lower plane, such as that occupied while one is engaged in the solution of the problems of business and professional routine.

When lifted to this higher level of thought, through any form of mind stimulation, an individual occupies, relatively, the same position as one who has ascended in an airplane to a height from which he may see over and beyond the horizon line which limits his vision, while on the ground. Moreover, while on this higher level of thought, the individual is not hampered or bound by any of the stimuli which circumscribe and limit his vision while wrestling with the problems of gaining the three basic necessities of food, clothing, and shelter. He is in a world of thought in which the ORDINARY, work-a-day thoughts have been as effectively removed as are the hills and valleys and other limitations of physical vision, when he rises in an airplane.

While on this exalted plane of THOUGHT, the creative faculty of the mind is given freedom for action. The way has been cleared for the sixth sense to function, it becomes receptive to ideas which could not reach the individual under any other circumstances. The "sixth sense" is the faculty which marks the difference between a genius and an ordinary individual.

The creative faculty becomes more alert and receptive to vibrations, originating outside the individual's subconscious mind, the more this faculty is used, and the more the individual relies upon it, and makes demands upon it for thought impulses. This faculty can be cultivated and developed only through use. That which is known as ones conscience operates entirely through the faculty of the sixth sense.

The great artists, writers, musicians, and poets become great, because they acquire the habit of relying upon the "still small voice" which speaks from within, through the faculty of creative imagi-nation. It is a fact well known to people who have "keen" imaginations that their best ideas come through so-called "hunches."

There is a great orator who does not attain to greatness, until he closes his eyes and begins to rely entirely upon the faculty of Creative Imagination. When asked why he closed his eyes just be-fore the climaxes of his oratory, he replied, "I do it, because, then I speak through ideas which come to me from within."

One of America's financiers followed the habit of closing his eyes for two or three minutes before making a decision. When asked why he did this, he replied, "With my eyes closed, I am able to draw upon a source of superior intelligence."

It is a fact well known to psychologists that there is a very close relationship between sex desires and spiritual urges—a fact which accounts for the peculiar behavior of people who participate in the orgies known as religious "revivals," common among the primitive types.

The world is ruled, and the destiny of civilization is established, by the human emotions. People are influenced in their actions, not by reason so much as by "feelings." The creative faculty of the mind is set into action entirely by emotions, and not by cold reason. The most powerful of all human emotions is that of sex. There are other mind stimulants, some of which have been listed, but no one of them, nor all of them combined, can equal the driving power of sex. A mind stimulant is any influence which will either temporarily, or permanently, increase the vibrations of thought. The ten major stimulants, described, are those most commonly resorted to. Through these sources one may commune with In.-finite Intelligence, or enter, at will, the storehouse of the subconscious mind, either one's own, or that of another person, a procedure which is all there is of genius.

Most people can be influenced only through an appeal to their emotions. The factor of personality known as "personal magnetism" is nothing more nor less than sex energy. Highly sexed people always have a plentiful supply of magnetism. Through cultivation and understanding, this vital force may be drawn upon and used to great advantage in the relationships between people. This energy may be communicated to others through the following media:

1. The hand-shake. The touch of the hand indicates, instantly, the presence of magnetism, or the lack of it.

2. The tone of voice. Magnetism, or sex energy, is the factor with which the voice may be colored, or made musical and charming.

3. Posture and carriage of the body. Highly sexed people move briskly, and with grace and ease.

4. The vibrations of thought. Highly sexed people mix the emotion of sex with their thoughts, or may do so at will, and in that way, may influence those around them.

5. Body adornment. People who are highly sexed are usually very careful about their personal appearance. They usually select clothing of a style becoming to their personality, physique, complexion, etc.

Transmutation of sex energy calls for more will power than the average person cares to use for this purpose. Those who find it difficult to summon will-power sufficient for transmutation, may gradually acquire this ability. Though this requires will-power, the reward for the practice is more than worth the effort.

The entire subject of sex is one with which the majority of people appear to be unpardonably ignorant. The urge of sex has been grossly misunderstood, slandered, and burlesqued by the ignorant and the evil minded, for so long that the very word sex is seldom used in polite society. Men and women who are known to be blessed — yes, BLESSED — with highly sexed natures, are usually looked upon as being people who will bear watching. Instead of being called blessed, they are usually called cursed.

Millions of people, even in this age of enlightenment, have inferiority complexes which they developed because of this false belief that a highly sexed nature is a curse. The emotion of sex is a virtue when used intelligently, and with discrimination. It may be misused, and often is, to such an extent that it debases, instead of enriches, both body and mind.

Nature begins to harmonize the emotions of love and sex in the individual, mostly between the ages of thirty and forty, so that he may draw upon these great forces, and apply them jointly as stimuli to action. Sex, alone, is a mighty urge to action, but its forces are like a cyclone-they are often uncontrollable. When the emotion of love begins to mix itself with the emotion of sex, the result is calmness of purpose, poise, accuracy of judgment, and balance.

Reformation comes, if at all, through the heart, or the emotional side of man, not through his head, or reasoning side. Reformation means, "a change of heart." It does not mean a "change of head." A man may, because of reason, make certain changes in his personal conduct to avoid the consequences of undesirable effects, but GENUINE REFORMATION comes only through a change of heart-through a DESIRE to change.

Love, Romance, and Sex are all emotions capable of driving men to heights of super achievement. Love is the emotion which serves as a safety valve, and insures balance, poise, and constructive effort. When combined, these three emotions may lift one to an altitude of a genius.

The road to genius consists of the development, control, and use of sex, love, and romance. Briefly, the process may be stated as follows:

Encourage the presence of these emotions as the dominating thoughts in one's mind, and discourage the presence of all the destructive emotions. The mind is a creature of habit. It thrives upon the dominating thoughts fed it. Through the faculty of will-power, one may discourage the presence of any emotion, and encourage the presence of any other. Control of the mind, through the power of will, is not difficult. Control comes from persistence, and habit. The secret of control lies in understanding the process of transmutation. When any negative emotion presents itself in one's mind, it can be transmuted into a positive, or constructive emotion, by the simple procedure of changing one's thoughts.

The emotions of love and sex leave their unmistakable marks upon the features. Moreover, these signs are so visible, that all who wish may read them. The man who is driven by the storm of passion, based upon sex desires alone, plainly advertises that fact to the entire world, by the expression of his eyes, and the lines of his face. The emotion of love, when mixed with the emotion of sex, softens, modifies, and beautifies the facial expression. No character analyst is needed to tell you this — you may observe it for yourself.

The emotion of love brings out, and develops, the artistic and the aesthetic nature of man. It leaves its impress upon one's very soul, even after the fire has been subdued by time and circum-stance.

Memories of love never pass. They linger, guide, and influence long after the source of stimulation has faded. There is nothing new in this. Every person, who has been moved by GENUINE LOVE, knows that it leaves enduring traces upon the human heart. The effect of love endures, because love is spiritual in nature. The man who cannot be stimulated to great heights by love, is hopeless – he is dead, though he may seem to live.

Even the memories of love are sufficient to lift one to a higher plane of creative effort. The major force of love may spend itself and pass away, like a fire which has burned itself out, but it leaves be-hind indelible marks as evidence that it passed that way. Its departure often prepares the human heart for a still greater love.

Go back into your yesterdays, at times, and bathe your mind in the beautiful memories of past love. It will soften the influence of the present worries and annoyances. It will give you a source of escape from the unpleasant realities of life, and maybe—who knows?—your mind will yield to you, during this temporary retreat into the world of fantasy, ideas, or plans which may change the entire financial or spiritual status of your life.

If you believe yourself unfortunate, because you have "loved and lost," perish the thought. One who has loved truly, can never lose entirely. Love is whimsical and temperamental. Its nature is ephemeral, and transitory. It comes when it pleases, and goes away without warning. Accept and enjoy it while it remains, but spend no time worrying about its departure. Worry will never bring it back.

Dismiss, also, the thought that love never comes but once. Love may come and go, times without number, but there are no two love experiences which affect one in just the same way. There may be, and there usually is, one love experience which leaves a deeper imprint on the heart than all the others, but all love experiences are beneficial, except to the person who becomes resentful and cynical when love makes its departure.

There should be no disappointment over love, and there would be none if people understood the difference between the emotions of love and sex. The major difference is that love is spiritual, while sex is biological. No experience, which touches the human heart with a spiritual force, can possibly be harmful, except through ignorance, or jealousy.

Love is, without question, life's greatest experience. It brings one into communion with Infinite Intelligence. When mixed with the emotions of romance and sex, it may lead one far up the ladder of creative effort. The emotions of love, sex, and romance, are sides of the eternal triangle of achievement-building genius. Nature creates genii through no other force.

When the emotion of romance is added to those of love and sex, the obstructions between the finite mind of man and Infinite Intelligence are removed. Then a genius has been born!

Man's greatest motivating force is his desire to please woman! Men who accumulate large fortunes, and attain to great heights of power and fame, do so, mainly, to satisfy their desire to please women. Take women out of their lives, and great wealth would be useless to most men. The woman who understands man's nature and tactfully caters to it, need have no fear of competition from other women. Men may be "giants" with indomitable will-power when dealing with other men, but they are easily managed by the women of their choice. Most men will not admit that they are easily influenced by the women they prefer, because it is in the nature of the male to want to be recognized as the stronger of the species. Moreover, the intelligent woman recognizes this "manly trait" and very wisely makes no issue of it.

Some men know that they are being influenced by the women of their choice—their wives, sweethearts, mothers or sisters—but they tactfully refrain from rebelling against the influence because they are intelligent enough to know that NO MAN IS HAPPY OR COMPLETE WITHOUT THE MODIFYING INFLUENCE OF THE RIGHT WOMAN. The man who does not recognize this important truth deprives himself of the power which has done more to help men achieve success than all other forces combined.

CHAPTER 12
THE SUBCONSCIOUS MIND

THE CONNECTING LINK

The Eleventh Step toward Riches

THE SUBCONSCIOUS MIND consists of a field of consciousness, in which every impulse of thought that reaches the objective mind through any of the five senses, is classified and recorded, and from which thoughts may be recalled or withdrawn as letters may be taken from a filing cabinet.

It receives, and files, sense impressions or thoughts, regardless of their nature. You may VOLUNTARILY plant in your subconscious mind any plan, thought, or purpose which you desire to translate into its physical equivalent. The subconscious acts first on the dominating desires which have been mixed with emotional feeling, such as faith.

Consider this in connection with the instructions given in the chapter on DESIRE, for taking the six steps there outlined, and the instructions given in the chapter on the building and execution of plans, and you will understand the importance of the thought conveyed.

THE SUBCONSCIOUS MIND WORKS DAY AND NIGHT. Through a method of procedure, unknown to man, the subconscious mind draws upon the forces of Infinite Intelligence for the power with which it voluntarily transmutes one's desires into their physical equivalent, making use, always of the most practical media by which this end may be accomplished.

You cannot entirely control your subconscious mind, but you can voluntarily hand over to it any plan, desire, or purpose which you wish transformed into concrete form. Read, again, instructions for using the subconscious mind, in the chapter on autosuggestion.

There is plenty of evidence to support the belief that the subconscious mind is the connecting link between the finite mind of man and Infinite Intelligence. It is the intermediary through which one may draw upon the forces of Infinite Intelligence at will. It, alone, contains the secret process by which mental impulses are modified and changed into their spiritual equivalent. It, alone, is the medium through which prayer may be transmitted to the source capable of answering prayer. The possibilities of creative effort connected with the subconscious mind are stupendous and imponderable. They inspire one with awe. The suggestion that the subconscious mind is the medium of communication between the thinking mind of man and Infinite Intelligence is, of itself, a thought which almost paralyzes one's reason.

After you have accepted, as a reality, the existence of the subconscious mind, and understand its possibilities, as a medium for transmuting your DESIRES into their physical equivalent, you will comprehend the full significance of the instructions given in the chapter on DESIRE. You will also understand why you have been repeatedly admonished to MAKE YOUR DESIRES CLEAR, AND TO REDUCE THEM TO WRITING. You will also understand the necessity of PERSISTENCE in carrying out instructions.

The thirteen principles are the stimuli with which you acquire the ability to reach, and to influence your subconscious mind. Do not become discouraged, if you cannot do this upon the first attempt. Remember that the subconscious mind may be voluntarily directed only through habit, under the directions given in the chapter on FAITH. You have not yet had time to master faith. Be patient. Be persistent.

A good many statements in the chapters on faith and auto-suggestion will be repeated here, for the benefit of YOUR subconscious mind. Remember, your subconscious mind functions voluntarily, whether you make any effort to influence it or not. This, naturally, suggests to you that thoughts of fear and poverty, and all negative thoughts serve as stimuli to your subconscious mind, unless, you master these impulses and give it more desirable food upon which it may feed.

The subconscious mind will not remain idle! If you fail to plant DESIRES in your subconscious mind, it will feed upon the thoughts which reach it as the result of your neglect. We have already explained that thought impulses, both negative and positive are reaching the subconscious mind continuously, from the four sources which were mentioned in the chapter on Sex Transmutation.

For the present, it is sufficient if you remember that you are living daily, in the midst of all manner of thought impulses which are reaching your subconscious mind, without your knowledge. Some of these impulses are negative, some are positive. You are now engaged in trying to help shut out the flow of negative impulses, and to aid in voluntarily influencing your subconscious mind, through positive impulses of DESIRE.

When you achieve this, you will possess the key which unlocks the door to your subconscious mind. Moreover, you will control that door so completely, that no undesirable thought may influence your subconscious mind.

Everything which man creates, BEGINS in the form of a thought impulse. Man can create nothing which he does not first conceive in THOUGHT. Through the aid of the imagination, thought impulses may be assembled into plans. The imagination, when under control, may be used for the creation of plans or purposes that lead to success in one's chosen occupation.

From these statements, you will readily observe that voluntary use of the subconscious mind calls for coordination and application of all the principles. Ella Wheeler Wilcox gave evidence of her understanding of the power of the subconscious mind when she wrote:

"You never can tell what a thought will do

In bringing you hate or love —

For thoughts are things, and their airy wings

Are swifter than carrier doves.

They follow the law of the universe —

Each thing creates its kind,

And they speed O'er the track to bring you back

Whatever went out from your mind."

Mrs. Wilcox understood the truth, that thoughts which go out from one's mind, also imbed themselves deeply in one's subconscious mind, where they serve as a magnet, pattern, or blueprint by which the subconscious mind is influenced while translating them into their physical equivalent. Thoughts are truly things, for the reason that every material thing begins in the form of thought-energy.

The subconscious mind is more susceptible to influence by impulses of thought mixed with "feeling" or emotion, than by those originating solely in the reasoning portion of the mind. In fact, there is much evidence to support the theory, that ONLY emotionalized thoughts have any ACTION influence upon the subconscious mind. It is a well known fact that emotion or feeling, rules the majority of people. If it is true that the subconscious mind responds more quickly to, and is influenced more readily by thought impulses which are well mixed with emotion, it is essential to become familiar with the more important of the emotions. There are seven major positive emotions, and seven major negative emotions. The negatives voluntarily inject themselves into the thought impulses, which insure passage into the subconscious mind. The positives must be injected, through the principle of auto-suggestion, into the thought impulses which an individual wishes to pass on to his subconscious mind. (Instructions have been given in the chapter on auto-suggestion.)

These emotions, or feeling impulses, may be likened to yeast in a loaf of bread, because they constitute the ACTION element, which transforms thought impulses from the passive to the active state. Thus may one understand why thought impulses, which have been well mixed with emotion, are acted upon more readily than thought impulses originating in "cold reason."

Note: "cold reason" can be paralyzing, "freezing", just as fear is. The majority of "reasons" are the ones inspired by fear and other non-adaptive emotional states. Reason strives for security, continuity and status quo. Those are the major obstacles to development and change, and to fulfillment of one's desires, whatever direction these desires are pointing.

You are preparing yourself to influence and control the "inner audience" of your subconscious mind, in order to hand over to it the DESIRE for money, which you wish transmuted into its physical equivalent. It is essential, therefore, that you understand the method of approach to this "inner audience." You must speak its language, or it will not heed your call. It understands best the language of emotion or feeling. Let us, therefore describe here the seven major positive emotions, and the seven major negative emotions, so that you may draw upon the positives, and avoid the negatives, when giving instructions to your subconscious mind.

Major positive emotions include desire, belief, love, sex, enthusiasm, romance and hope. Major negative emotions include fear, jealousy, hatred, revenge, greed, superstition and anger.

Positive and negative emotions cannot occupy the mind at the same time. One or the other must dominate. It is your responsibility to make sure that positive emotions constitute the dominating influence of your mind. Here the law of HABIT will come to your aid. Form the habit of applying and using the positive emotions! Eventually, they will dominate your mind so completely, that the negatives cannot enter it.

Note: some of the emotions traditionally viewed as destructive, such as anger, are not destructive as long as you do not act destructively on them (this includes feeding thoughts of revenge or other mind-destructive attitudes). The emotion of anger becomes "positive" when it replaces despair, fear or shame, which are even more negative. It becomes positive when it leads to positive solutions, aimed at reducing tensions and making better progress. It becomes positive when it motivates you to act positively towards your goals, and not aggressively towards other people. In the book Power vs. Force by David R. Hawkins, there's a hierarchy of levels of human consciousness, each of the levels corresponding to an emotion, from shame at the bottom to peace at the top. Every emotion, whatever negative, can be positive in relation to the previous one, and can indicate positive change.

THE POWER OF PRAYER

If you are an observing person, you must have noticed that most people resort to prayer ONLY after everything else has FAILED! Or else they pray by a ritual of meaningless words. And, because it is a fact that most people who pray, do so ONLY AFTER EVERYTHING ELSE HAS FAILED, they go to prayer with their minds filled with FEAR and DOUBT, which are the emotions the subconscious mind acts upon, and passes on to Infinite Intelligence. Likewise, that is the emotion which Infinite Intelligence receives, and ACTS UPON.

If you pray for a thing, but have fear as you pray, that you may not receive it, or that your prayer will not be acted upon by Infinite Intelligence, your prayer will have been in vain.

Prayer does, sometimes, result in the realization of that for which one prays. If you have ever had the experience of receiving that for which YOU prayed, go back in your memory, and recall your actual STATE OF MIND, while you were praying, and you will know, for sure, that the theory here described is more than a theory.

The time will come when the schools and educational institutions of the country will teach the "science of prayer." Moreover, then prayer may be, and will be reduced to a science. When that time comes, (it will come as soon as mankind is ready for it, and demands it), no one will approach the Universal Mind in a state of fear, for the very good reason that there will be no such emotion as fear. Ignorance, superstition, and false teaching will have disappeared, and man will have attained his true status as a child of Infinite Intelligence. A few have already attained this blessing.

If you believe this prophesy is far-fetched, take a look at the human race in retrospect. Less than a hundred years ago, men believed the lightning to be evidence of the wrath of God, and feared it. Now, thanks to the power of FAITH, men have harnessed the lightning and made it turn the wheels of industry.

Much less than a hundred years ago, men believed the space between the planets to be nothing but a great void, a stretch of dead nothingness. Now, thanks to this same power of FAITH, men know that far from being either dead or a void, the space between the planets is very much alive, that it is the highest form of vibration known, excepting, perhaps, the vibration of THOUGHT. Moreover, men know that this living, pulsating, vibratory energy which permeates every atom of matter, and fills every niche of space, connects every human brain with every other human brain.

What reason have men to believe that this same energy does not connect every human brain with Infinite Intelligence?

There are no toll-gates between the finite mind of man and Infinite Intelligence. The communication costs nothing except Patience, Faith, Persistence, Understanding, and a SINCERE DESIRE to communicate. Moreover, the approach can be made only by the individual himself. Paid prayers are worthless. Infinite Intelligence does no business by proxy. You either go direct, or you do not communicate.

Thoughts which you wish to communicate to Infinite Intelligence, must undergo transformation, such as can be given only through your own subconscious mind.

The method by which you may communicate with Infinite Intelligence is very similar to that through which the vibration of sound is communicated by radio. If you understand the working principle of radio, you of course, know that sound cannot be communicated through the ether until it has been "stepped up," or changed into a rate of vibration which the human ear cannot detect. The radio sending station picks up the sound of the human voice, and modifies it by stepping up the vibration millions of times. Only in this way, can the vibration of sound be communicated through the ether. After this transformation has taken place, the ether "picks up" the energy (which originally was in the form of vibrations of sound), carries that energy to radio receiving stations, and these receiving sets "step" that energy back down to its original rate of vibration so it is recognized as sound.

The subconscious mind is the intermediary, which translates one's prayers into terms which Infinite Intelligence can recognize, presents the message, and brings back the answer in the form of a definite plan or idea for procuring the object of the prayer. Understand this principle, and you will know why mere words read from a prayer book cannot, and will never serve as an agency of communication between the mind of man and Infinite Intelligence.

Before your prayer will reach Infinite Intelligence (a statement of the author's theory only), it probably is transformed from its original thought vibration into terms of spiritual vibration. Faith is the only known agency which will give your thoughts a spiritual nature. FAITH and FEAR make poor bedfellows. Where one is found, the other cannot exist.

Note: Gregg Braden in his book "The Secrets of the Lost Mode of Prayer" advocates a similar idea of feeling being the substance of the prayer and the very thing you will subsequently receive (like creates like). He advises to be continuously "praying" by noticing "the beauty you live by", that will be reflected back to you in form of circumstances of your life.

CHAPTER 13
THE BRAIN

A BROADCASTING AND RECEIVING STATION FOR THOUGHT

The Twelfth Step toward Riches

Dr. Alexander Graham Bell and Dr. Elmer R. Gates, observed that every human brain is both a broadcasting and receiving station for the vibration of thought.

Through the medium of the ether, in a fashion similar to that employed by the radio broadcasting principle, every human brain is capable of picking up vibrations of thought which are being released by other brains.

In connection with the statement in the preceding paragraph, compare, and consider the description of the Creative Imagination, as outlined in the chapter on Imagination. The Creative Imagination is the "receiving set" of the brain, which receives thoughts, released by the brains of others. It is the agency of communication between one's conscious, or reasoning mind, and the four sources from which one may receive thought stimuli.

When stimulated, or "stepped up" to a high rate of vibration, the mind becomes more receptive to the vibration of thought which reaches it through the ether from outside sources. This "stepping up" process takes place through the positive emotions, or the negative emotions. Through the emotions, the vibrations of thought may be increased.

Vibrations of an exceedingly high rate are the only vibrations picked up and carried, by the ether, from one brain to another. Thought is energy travelling at an exceedingly high rate of vibration. Thought, which has been modified or "stepped up" by any of the major emotions, vibrates at a much higher rate than ordinary thought, and it is this type of thought which passes from one brain to another, through the broadcasting machinery of the human brain.

The emotion of sex stands at the head of the list of human emotions, as far as intensity and driving force are concerned. The brain which has been stimulated by the emotion of sex, vibrates at a much more rapid rate than it does when that emotion is quiescent or absent.

The result of sex transmutation, is the increase of the rate of vibration of thoughts to such a pitch that the Creative Imagination becomes highly receptive to ideas, which it picks up from the ether. On the other hand, when the brain is vibrating at a rapid rate, it not only attracts thoughts and ideas released by other brains through the medium of the ether, but it gives to one's own thoughts that "feeling" which is essential before those thoughts will be picked up and acted upon by one's subconscious mind.

Thus, you will see that the broadcasting principle is the factor through which you mix feeling, or emotion with your thoughts and pass them on to your subconscious mind.

The subconscious mind is the "sending station" of the brain, through which vibrations of thought are broadcast. The Creative Imagination is the "receiving set," through which the vibrations of thought are picked up from the ether.

Along with the important factors of the subconscious mind, and the faculty of the Creative Imagination, which constitute the sending and receiving sets of your mental broadcasting machinery, consider now the principle of auto-suggestion, which is the medium by which you may put into operation your "broadcasting" station.

Operation of your mental "broadcasting" station is a comparatively simple procedure. You have but three principles to bear in mind, and to apply, when you wish to use your broadcasting station—the SUBCONSCIOUS MIND, CREATIVE IMAGINATION, and AUTO-SUGGESTION. The stimuli through which you put these three principles into action have been described—the procedure begins with DESIRE.

THE GREATEST FORCES ARE "INTANGIBLE"

Through the ages which have passed, man has depended too much upon his physical senses, and has limited his knowledge to physical things, which he could see, touch, weigh, and measure. We are now entering the most marvelous of all ages—an age which will teach us something of the intangible forces of the world about us. Perhaps we shall learn, as we pass through this age, that the "other self" is more powerful than the physical self we see when we look into a mirror.

Sometimes men speak lightly of the intangibles— the things which they cannot perceive through any of their five senses, and when we hear them, it should remind us that all of us are controlled by forces which are unseen and intangible.

THE DRAMATIC STORY OF THE BRAIN

Last, but not least, man, with all of his boasted culture and education, understands little or nothing of the intangible force (the greatest of all the intangibles) of thought. He knows but little concerning the physical brain, and its vast network of intricate machinery through which the power of thought is translated into its material equivalent, but he is now entering an age which shall yield enlightenment on the subject.

After this book had been written, just before the manuscript went to the publisher, there appeared in the New York Times, an editorial showing that at least one great University, and one intelligent investigator in the field of mental phenomena, are carrying on an organized research through which conclusions have been reached that parallel many of those described in this and the following chapter. The editorial briefly analyzed the work carried on by Dr. Rhine, and his associates at Duke University: "What is 'Telepathy'?

"A month ago we cited on this page some of the remarkable results achieved by Professor Rhine and his associates in Duke University from more than a hundred thousand tests to determine the existence of 'telepathy' and 'clairvoyance.' These results were summarized in the first two articles in Harpers Magazine. In the second which has now appeared, the author, E. H. Wright, attempts to summarize what has been learned, or what it seems reasonable to infer, regarding the exact nature of these 'extrasensory' modes of perception.

"The actual existence of telepathy and clairvoyance now seems to some scientists enormously probable as the result of Rhine's experiments. Various percipients were asked to name as many cards in a special pack as they could without looking at them and without other sensory access to them. About a score of men and women were discovered who could regularly name so many of the cards correctly that 'there was not one chance in many a million million of their having done their feats by luck or accident.'

"But how did they do them? These powers, assuming that they exist, do not seem to be sensory. There is no known organ for them. The experiments worked just as well at distances of several hundred miles as they did in the same room. These facts also dispose, in Mr. Wright's opinion, of the attempt to explain telepathy or clairvoyance through any physical theory of radiation. All known forms of radiant energy decline inversely as the square of the distance traversed. Telepathy and clairvoyance do not. But they do vary through physical causes as our other mental powers do. Contrary to widespread opinion, they do not improve when the percipient is asleep or half-asleep, but, on the contrary, when he is most wide-awake and alert. Rhine discovered that a narcotic will invariably lower a percipient's score, while a stimulant will always send it higher. The most reliable performer apparently cannot make a good score unless he tries to do his best.

"One conclusion that Wright draws with some confidence is that telepathy and clairvoyance are really one and the same gift. That is, the faculty that 'sees' a card face down on a table seems to be exactly the same one that 'reads' a thought residing only in another mind. There are several grounds for believing this. So far, for example, the two gifts have been found in every person who enjoys either of them. In every one so far the two have been of equal vigor, almost exactly. Screens, walls, distances, have no effect at all on either. Wright advances from this conclusion to express what he puts forward as no more than the mere 'hunch' that other extra-sensory experiences, prophetic dreams, premonitions of disaster, and the like, may also prove to be part of the same faculty. The reader is not asked to accept any of these conclusions unless he finds it necessary, but the evidence that Rhine has piled up must remain impressive."

In view of Dr. Rhine's announcement in connection with the conditions under which the mind responds to what he terms "extra—sensory modes of perception, I now feel privileged to add to his testimony by stating that my associates and I have discovered what we believe to be the ideal conditions under which the mind can be stimulated so that the sixth sense described in the next chapter, can be made to function in a practical way.

The conditions to which I refer consist of a close working alliance between myself and two members of my staff. Through experimentation and practice, we have discovered how to stimulate our minds (by applying the principle used in connection with the "Invisible Counselors" described in the next chapter) so that we can, by a process of blending our three minds into one, find the solution to a great variety of personal problems which are submitted by my clients.

The procedure is very simple. We sit down at a conference table, clearly state the nature of the problem we have under consideration, then begin discussing it. Each contributes whatever thoughts that may occur. The strange thing about this method of mind stimulation is that it places each participant in communication with unknown sources of knowledge definitely outside his own experience. If you understand the principle described in the chapter on the Master Mind, you of course recognize the round-table procedure here described as being a practical application of the Master Mind. This method of mind stimulation, through harmonious discussion of definite subjects, between three people, illustrates the simplest and most practical use of the Master Mind.

CHAPTER 14
THE SIXTH SENSE

THE DOOR TO THE TEMPLE OF WISDOM

The Thirteenth Step toward Riches

THE "thirteenth" principle is known as the SIXTH SENSE, through which Infinite Intelligence may, and will communicate voluntarily, without any effort from, or demands by, the individual. This Intelligence may, through the principles of this philosophy, be induced to aid in transmuting DESIRES into concrete, or material form. The author has this knowledge, because he has experimented with it— and has EXPERIENCED IT.

This principle is the apex of the philosophy. It can be assimilated, understood, and applied ONLY by first mastering the other twelve principles.

The SIXTH SENSE is that portion of the subconscious mind which has been referred to as the Creative Imagination. It has also been referred to as the "receiving set" through which ideas, plans, and thoughts flash into the mind. The "flashes" are sometimes called "hunches" or "inspirations."

Understanding of the sixth sense comes only by meditation through mind development from within. The sixth sense probably is the medium of contact between the finite mind of man and Infinite Intelligence, and for this reason, it is a mixture of both the mental and the spiritual. It is believed to be the point at which the mind of man contacts the Universal Mind.

Through the aid of the sixth sense, you will be warned of impending dangers in time to avoid them, and notified of opportunities in time to embrace them.

If you have mastered each of the preceding principles, you are now prepared to accept, without being skeptical, the stupendous claims made here. If you have not mastered the other principles, you must do so before you may determine, definitely, whether or not the claims made in this chapter are fact or fiction.

There comes to your aid, and to do your bidding, with the development of the sixth sense, a "guardian angel" who will open to you at all times the door to the Temple of Wisdom.

The author is not a believer in, nor an advocate of "miracles," for the reason that he has enough knowledge of Nature to understand that Nature never deviates from her established laws. Some of her laws are so incomprehensible that they produce what appear to be "miracles." The sixth sense comes as near to being a miracle as anything I have ever experienced, and it appears so, only because I do not understand the method by which this principle is operated.

While I was passing through the age of "hero-worship" I found myself trying to imitate those whom I most admired. Moreover, I discovered that the element of FAITH, with which I endeavored to imitate my idols, gave me great capacity to do so quite successfully. I have never entirely divested myself of this habit of hero-worship, although I have passed the age commonly given over to such. My experience has taught me that the next best thing to being truly great, is to emulate the great, by feeling and action, as nearly as possible.

Long before I had ever written a line for publication, or endeavored to deliver a speech in public, I followed the habit of reshaping my own character, by trying to imitate the men whose lives and life-works had been most impressive to me.

Every night, over a long period of years, I held an imaginary Council meeting with this group whom I called my "Invisible Counselors." The procedure was this. Just before going to sleep at night, I would shut my eyes, and see, in my imagination, this group of men seated with me around my Council Table. Here I had not only an opportunity to sit among those whom I considered to be great, but I actually dominated the group, by serving as the Chairman.

I had a very DEFINITE PURPOSE in indulging my imagination through these nightly meetings. My purpose was to rebuild my own character so it would represent a composite of the characters of my imaginary counselors. Realizing, as I did, early in life, that I had to overcome the handicap of birth in an environment of ignorance and superstition, I deliberately assigned myself the task of voluntary rebirth through the method here described.

BUILDING CHARACTER THROUGH AUTO-SUGGESTION

Being an earnest student of psychology, I knew, of course, that all men have become what they are, because of their DOMINATING THOUGHTS AND DESIRES. I knew that every deeply seated desire has the effect of causing one to seek outward expression through which that desire may be transmuted into reality. I knew that self-suggestion is a powerful factor in building character, that it is, in fact, the sole principle through which character is built.

With this knowledge of the principles of mind operation, I was fairly well armed with the equipment needed in rebuilding my character. In these imaginary Council meetings I called on my Cabinet members for the knowledge I wished each to contribute, addressing myself to each member in audible words.

My method of addressing the members of the imaginary Cabinet would vary, according to the traits of character in which I was, for the moment, most interested in acquiring. I studied the records of their lives with painstaking care. After some months of this nightly procedure, I was astounded by the discovery that these imaginary figures became, apparently real.

After that, I began to add new members to my Cabinet, until now it consists of more than fifty, among them Christ, St. Paul, Galileo, Copernicus, Aristotle, Plato, Socrates, Homer, Voltaire, Bruno,

Spinoza, Kant, Schopenhauer, Newton, Confucius, and William James.

During my meetings with the "Invisible Counselors" I find my mind most receptive to ideas, thoughts, and knowledge which reach me through the sixth sense. I can truthfully say that I owe entirely to my "Invisible Counselors" full credit for such ideas, facts, or knowledge as I received through "inspiration."

! Your own thoughts and DESIRES serve as the magnet which attracts units of life, from the great ocean of life out there. Only the friendly units are attracted—the ones which harmonize with the nature of your DESIRES!

This is the first time that I have had the courage to mention this. Heretofore, I have remained quiet on the subject, because I knew, from my own attitude in connection with such matters, that I would be misunderstood if I described my unusual experience. I have been emboldened now to reduce my experience to the printed page, because I am now less concerned about what "they say" than I was in the years that have passed. One of the blessings of maturity is that it sometimes brings one greater courage to be truthful, regardless of what those who do not understand, may think or say.

Somewhere in the cell-structure of the brain, is located an organ which receives vibrations of thought ordinarily called "hunches." So far, science has not discovered where this organ of the sixth sense is located, but this is not important. The fact remains that human beings do receive accurate knowledge, through sources other than the physical senses. Such knowledge, generally, is received when the mind is under the influence of extraordinary stimulation. Any emergency which arouses the emotions, and causes the heart to beat more rapidly than normal may, and generally does, bring the sixth sense into action.

On scores of occasions, when I have faced emergencies, some of them so grave that my life was in jeopardy, I have been miraculously guided past these difficulties through the influence of my "Invisible Counselors."

My original purpose in conducting Council meetings with imaginary beings, was solely that of impressing my own subconscious mind, through the principle of auto-suggestion, with certain characteristics which I desired to acquire. In more recent years, my experimentation has taken on an entirely different trend. I now go to my imaginary counselors with every difficult problem which confronts me and my clients. The results are often astonish-ing, although I do not depend entirely on this form of Counsel.

You, of course, have recognized that this chapter covers a subject with which a majority of people are not familiar. The Sixth Sense is a subject that will be of great interest and benefit to the person whose aim is to accumulate vast wealth, but it need not claim the attention of those whose desires are more modest.

Nearly all great leaders understood, and probably made use of the sixth sense almost continuously. The major portion of their greatness consisted of their knowledge of this principle.

The sixth sense is not something that one can take off and put on at will. Ability to use this great power comes slowly, through application of the other principles outlined in this book. Seldom does any individual come into workable knowledge of the sixth sense before the age of forty. More often the knowledge is not available until one is well past fifty, and this, for the reason that the spiritual forces, with which the sixth sense is so closely related, do not mature and become usable except through years of meditation, self-examination, and serious thought.

No matter who you are, or what may have been your purpose in reading this book, you can profit by it without understanding the principle described in this chapter. The chapter on the sixth sense was included, because the book is designed for the purpose of presenting a complete philosophy by which individuals may unerringly guide themselves in attaining whatever they ask of life. The starting point of all achievement is DESIRE. The finishing point is that brand of KNOWLEDGE which leads to understanding—understanding of self, understanding of others, understanding of the laws of Nature, recognition and understanding of HAPPINESS.

This sort of understanding comes in its fullness only through familiarity with, and use of the principle of the sixth sense, hence that principle had to be included as a part of this philosophy, for the benefit of those who demand more than money.

Having read the chapter, you must have observed that while reading it, you were lifted to a high level of mental stimulation. Splendid! Come back to this again a month from now, read it once more, and observe that your mind will soar to a still higher level of stimulation. Repeat this experience from time to time, giving no concern as to how much or how little you learn at the time, and eventually you will find yourself in possession of a power that will enable you to throw off discouragement, master fear, overcome procrastination, and draw freely upon your imagination. Then you will have felt the touch of that unknown "something" which has been the moving spirit of every truly great thinker leader, artist, musician, writer, statesman. Then you will be in position to transmute your DESIRES into their physical or financial counterpart as easily as you may lie down and quit at the first sign of opposition.

CHAPTER 15
HOW TO OUTWIT THE SIX GHOSTS OF FEAR

Take Inventory of Yourself, As You Read This Closing Chapter, and Find Out How Many of the "Ghosts" Are Standing in Your Way

FAITH VS. FEAR!

Here will be found a full description of the six fears which are the cause of all discouragement, timidity, procrastination, indifference, indecision, and the lack of ambition, self-reliance, initiative, self-control, and enthusiasm. Search yourself carefully as you study these six enemies, as they may exist only in your subconscious mind, where their presence will be hard to detect. Remember, too, as you analyze the "Six Ghosts of Fear," that they are nothing but ghosts because they exist only in one's mind. Remember, also, that ghosts—creations of uncontrolled imagination—have caused most of the damage people have done to their own minds, therefore, ghosts can be as dangerous as if they lived and walked on the earth in physical bodies.

BEFORE you can put any portion of this philosophy into successful use, your mind must be prepared to receive it. The preparation is not difficult. It begins with study, analysis, and understanding of three enemies which you shall have to clear out. These are INDECISION, DOUBT, and FEAR!

The Sixth Sense will never function while these three negatives, or any of them remain in your mind. The members of this unholy trio are closely related; where one is found, the other two are close at hand.

INDECISION is the seedling of FEAR! Remember this, as you read. Indecision crystalizes into DOUBT, the two blend and become FEAR! The "blending" process often is slow. This is one reason why these three enemies are so dangerous. They germinate and grow without their presence being observed.

This chapter describes an **end** which must be attained before the philosophy, as a whole, can be put into practical use. It also analyzes a condition which has, but lately, reduced huge numbers of people to poverty, and it states a truth which must be understood by all who accumulate riches, whether measured in terms of money or a state of mind of far greater value than money. The purpose of this chapter is to turn the spotlight of attention upon the cause and the cure of the six basic fears. Before we can master an enemy, we must know its name, its habits, and its place of abode. As you read, analyze yourself carefully, and determine which, if any, of the six common fears have attached themselves to you. Sometimes they remain hidden in the subconscious mind, where they are difficult to locate, and still more difficult to eliminate.

THE SIX BASIC FEARS

There are six basic fears, with some combination of which every human suffers at one tune or another. Most people are fortunate if they do not suffer from the entire six. Named in the order of their most common appearance, they are:

The fear of POVERTY

The fear of CRITICISM

The fear of ILL HEALTH

The fear of LOSS OF LOVE OF SOMEONE

The fear of OLD AGE

The fear of DEATH

All other fears are of minor importance, they can be grouped under these six headings.

Fears are nothing more than states of mind. One's state of mind is subject to control and direction.

Man can create nothing which he does not first conceive in the form of an impulse of thought. Following this statement, comes another of still greater importance, namely, MAN'S THOUGHT IM-PULSES BEGIN IMMEDIATELY TO TRANSLATE THEMSELVES INTO THEIR PHYSICAL EQUIVALENT, WHETHER THOSE THOUGHTS ARE VOLUNTARY OR INVOLUNTARY. Thought impulses which are picked up through the ether, by mere chance (thoughts which have been released by other minds) may determine one's financial, business, professional, or social destiny just as surely as do the thought impulses which one creates by intent and design.

We are here laying the foundation for the presentation of a fact of great importance to the person who does not understand why some people appear to be "lucky" while others of equal or greater ability, training, experience, and brain capacity, seem destined to ride with misfortune. This fact may be explained by the statement that every human being has the ability to completely control his own mind, and with this control, obviously, every person may open his mind to the tramp thought impulses which are being released by other brains, or close the doors tightly and admit only thought impulses of his own choice.

Nature has endowed man with absolute control over but one thing, and that is THOUGHT. This fact, coupled with the additional fact that everything which man creates, begins in the form of a thought, leads one very near to the principle by which FEAR may be mastered.

If it is true that ALL THOUGHT HAS A TENDENCY TO CLOTHE ITSELF IN ITS PHYSICAL EQUIVALENT (and this is true, beyond any reasonable room for doubt), it is equally true that thought impulses of fear and poverty cannot be translated into terms of courage and financial gain.

THE FEAR OF POVERTY

This fear paralyzes the faculty of reason, destroys the faculty of imagination, kills off self-reliance, undermines enthusiasm, discourages initiative, leads to uncertainty of purpose, encourages procrastination, wipes out enthusiasm and makes self-control an impossibility. It takes the charm from one's personality, destroys the possibility of accurate thinking, diverts concentration of effort, it masters persistence, turns the will-power into nothingness, destroys ambition, beclouds the memory and invites failure in every conceivable form; it kills love and assassinates the finer emotions of the heart, discourages friendship and invites disaster in a hundred forms, leads to sleeplessness, misery and unhappiness—and all this despite the obvious truth that we live in a world of over-abundance of everything the heart could desire, with nothing standing between us and our desires, excepting lack of a definite purpose.

Fear of poverty is a state of mind, nothing else! But it is sufficient to destroy one's chances of achievement in any undertaking.

A new state of mind is something that one assumes. It cannot be purchased, it must be created.

The Fear of Poverty is, without doubt, the most destructive of the six basic fears. It has been placed at the head of the list, because it is the most difficult to master. Considerable courage is required to state the truth about the origin of this fear, and still greater courage to accept the truth after it has been stated. The fear of poverty grew out of man's inherited tendency to PREY UPON HIS FELLOW MAN ECONOMICALLY. Nearly all animals lower than man are motivated by instinct, but their capacity to "think" is limited, therefore, they prey upon one another physically. Man, with his superior sense of intuition, with the capacity to think and to reason, does not eat his fellowman bodily, he gets more satisfaction out of "eating" him FINANCIALLY. Man is so avaricious that every conceivable law has been passed to safeguard him from his fellowman.

It is no wonder that man fears poverty. Through a long line of inherited experiences man has learned, for sure, that some men cannot be trusted, where matters of money and earthly possessions are concerned. This is a rather stinging indictment, the worst part of it being that it is TRUE.

Self-analysis may disclose weaknesses which one does not like to acknowledge. The majority of people, if asked what they fear most, would reply, "I fear nothing." The reply would be inaccurate, because few people realize that they are bound, handicapped, whipped spiritually and physically through some form of fear. So subtle and deeply seated is the emotion of fear that one may go through life burdened with it, never recognizing its presence. Only a courageous analysis will disclose the presence of this universal enemy. When you begin such an analysis, search deeply into your character. Here is a list of the symptoms for which you should look:

SYMPTOMS OF THE FEAR OF POVERTY

❑ INDIFFERENCE. Commonly expressed through lack of ambition; willingness to tolerate poverty; acceptance of whatever compensation life may offer without protest; mental and physical laziness; lack of initiative, imagination, enthusiasm and self-control

❑ INDECISION. The habit of permitting others to do one's thinking. Staying "on the fence."

❑ DOUBT. Generally expressed through alibis and excuses designed to cover up, explain away, or apologize for one's failures, sometimes expressed in the form of envy of those who are successful, or by criticising them.

❑ WORRY. Usually expressed by finding fault with others, a tendency to spend beyond one's income, neglect of personal appearance, scowling and frowning; intemperance in the use of alcoholic drink, sometimes through the use of narcotics; nervousness, lack of poise, self-consciousness and lack of self-reliance.

❑ OVER-CAUTION. The habit of looking for the negative side of every circumstance, thinking and talking of possible failure instead of concentrating upon the means of succeeding. Knowing all the roads to disaster, but never searching for the plans to avoid failure. Wait ing for "the right time" to begin putting ideas and plans into action, until the waiting becomes a permanent habit. Remembering those who have failed, and forgetting those who have succeeded. Seeing the hole in the doughnut, but overlooking the doughnut. Pessimism, leading to indigestion, poor elimination, auto-intoxication, bad breath and bad disposition.

❏ PROCRASTINATION. The habit of putting off until tomorrow that which should have been done last year. Spending enough time in creating alibis and excuses to have done the job. This symptom is closely related to over-caution, doubt and worry. Refusal to accept responsibility when it can be avoided. Willingness to compromise rather than put up a stiff fight. Compromising with difficulties instead of harnessing and using them as stepping stones to advancement. Bargaining with Life for a penny, instead of demanding prosperity, opulence, riches, contentment and happiness. Planning what to do IF AND WHEN OVERTAKEN BY FAILURE, INSTEAD OF BURNING ALL BRIDGES AND MAKING RETREAT IMPOSSIBLE. Weakness of, and often total lack of self-confidence, definiteness of purpose, self-control, initiative, enthusiasm, ambition, thrift and sound reasoning ability.

❏ EXPECTING POVERTY INSTEAD OF DEMANDING RICHES. Association with those who accept poverty instead of seeking the company of those who demand and receive riches.

MONEY TALKS!

Some will ask, "Why did you write a book about money? Why measure riches in dollars, alone?" Some will believe, and rightly so, that there are other forms of riches more desirable than money. Yes, there are riches which cannot be measured in terms of dollars, but there are millions of people who will say, "Give me all the money I need, and I will find everything else I want." The major reason why I wrote this book on how to get money is the fact that the world has but lately passed through an experience that left millions of men and women paralyzed with the FEAR OF POVERTY. What this sort of fear does to one was well described by Westbrook Pegler, in the New York World-Telegram: "Money is only clam shells or metal discs or scraps of paper, and there are treasures of the heart and soul which money cannot buy, but most people, being broke, are unable to keep this in mind and sustain their spirits. When a man is down and out and on the street, unable to get any job at all, something happens to his spirit which can be observed in the droop of his shoulders, the set of his hat, his walk and his gaze. He cannot escape a feeling of inferiority among people with regular employment, even though he knows they are definitely not his equals in character, intelligence or ability. "These people—even his friends—feel, on the other hand, a sense of superiority and regard him, perhaps unconsciously, as a casualty. He may borrow for a time, but not enough to carry on in his accustomed way, and he cannot continue to borrow very long. But borrowing in itself, when a man is borrowing merely to live, is a depressing experience, and the money lacks the power of earned money to revive his spirits. Of course, none of this applies to bums or habitual ne'er-do-wells, but only to men of normal ambitions and self-respect.

"WOMEN CONCEAL DESPAIR. "Women in the same predicament must be different. We somehow do not think of women at all in considering the down-and-outers.

"MONEY MAKES DIFFERENCE. "He sees thousands of other people, bookkeepers or clerks or chemists or wagon hands, busy at their work and envies them from the bottom of his soul. They have their independence, their self-respect and manhood, and he simply cannot convince himself that he is a good man, too, though he argue it out and arrive at a favorable verdict hour after hour. "It is just money which makes this difference in him. With a little money he would be himself again.

THE FEAR OF CRITICISM

The fear of criticism takes on many forms. Let us now examine human behavior when this fear affects people in connection with the more important events of human relationship. Take for example practically any person who has reached the age of "mental maturity" (from 35 to 40 years of age, as a general average), and if you could read the secret thoughts of his mind, you would find a very decided disbelief in most of the fables taught by the majority of the dogmatists and theologians a few decades back. Not often, however, will you find a person who has the courage to openly state his belief on this subject. Most people will, if pressed far enough, tell a lie rather than admit that they do not believe the stories associated with that form of religion which held people in bondage prior to the age of scientific discovery and education.

Why does the average person, even in this day of enlightenment, shy away from denying his belief in the fables which were the basis of most of the religions a few decades ago? The answer is, "because of the fear of criticism." Men and women have been burned at the stake for daring to express disbelief. It is no wonder we have inherited a consciousness which makes us fear criticism. The time was, and not so far in the past, when criticism carried severe punishments – it still does in some countries.

The fear of criticism robs man of his initiative, destroys his power of imagination, limits his individuality, takes away his self-reliance, and does him damage in a hundred other ways. Parents often do their children irreparable injury by criticising them.

Criticism is the one form of service, of which everyone has too much. Everyone has a stock of it which is handed out, gratis, whether called for or not. One's nearest relatives often are the worst offenders. It should be recognized as a crime (in reality it is a crime of the worst nature), for any parent to build inferiority complexes in the mind of a child, through unnecessary criticism. Employers who understand human nature, get the best there is in men, not by criticism, but by constructive suggestion. Parents may accomplish the same results with their children. Criticism will plant FEAR in the human heart, or resentment, but it will not build love or affection.

SYMPTOMS OF THE FEAR OF CRITICISM

This fear is almost as universal as the fear of poverty, and its effects are just as fatal to personal achievement, mainly because this fear destroys initiative, and discourages the use of imagination. The major symptoms of the fear are:

❑ SELF-CONSCIOUSNESS. Generally expressed through nervousness, timidity in conversation and in meeting strangers, awkward movement of the hands and limbs, shifting of the eyes.

❑ LACK OF POISE. Expressed through lack of voice control, nervousness in the presence of others, poor posture of body, poor memory.

❑ PERSONALITY. Lacking in firmness of decision, personal charm, and ability to express opinions definitely. The habit of side-stepping issues instead of meeting them squarely. Agreeing with others without careful examination of their opinions.

❑ INFERIORITY COMPLEX. The habit of expressing self-approval by word of mouth and by actions, as a means of covering up a feeling of inferiority. Using "big words" to impress others, (often without knowing the real meaning of the words). Imitating others in dress, speech and manners. Boasting of imaginary achievements. This sometimes gives a surface appearance of a feeling of superiority.

❑ EXTRAVAGANCE. The habit of trying to "keep up with the Joneses," spending beyond one's income.

❑ LACK OF INITIATIVE. Failure to embrace opportunities for self-advancement, fear to express opinions, lack of confidence in one's own ideas, giving evasive answers to questions asked by superiors, hesitancy of manner and speech, deceit in both words and deeds.

❑ LACK OF AMBITION. Mental and physical laziness, lack of self-assertion, slowness in reaching decisions, easily influenced by others, the habit of criticising others behind their backs and flattering them to their faces, the habit of accepting defeat without protest, quitting an undertaking when opposed by others, suspicious of other people without cause, lacking in tact-fulness of manner and speech, unwillingness to accept the blame for mistakes.

THE FEAR OF ILL HEALTH

This fear may be traced to both physical and social heredity. It is closely associated, as to its origin, with the causes of fear of Old Age and the fear of Death, because it leads one closely to the border of "terrible worlds" of which man knows not, but concerning which he has been taught some discomforting stories. The opinion is somewhat general, also, that certain unethical people engaged in the business of "selling health" have had not a little to do with keeping alive the fear of ill health.

It has been shown most convincingly that the fear of disease, even where there is not the slightest cause for fear, often produces the physical symptoms of the disease feared. Powerful and mighty is the human mind! It builds or it destroys. Playing upon this common weakness of fear of ill health, dispensers of patent medicines have reaped fortunes.

There is overwhelming evidence that disease sometimes begins in the form of negative thought impulse. Such an impulse may be passed from one mind to another, by suggestion, or created by an individual in his own mind. A man who was blessed with more wisdom than this incident might indicate, once said "When anyone asks me how I feel, I always want to answer by knocking him down."

Doctors send patients into new climates for their health, because a change of "mental attitude" is necessary. The seed of fear of ill health lives in every human mind. Worry, fear, discouragement, disappointment in love and business affairs, cause this seed to germinate and grow.

Disappointments in business and in love stand at the head of the list of causes of fear of ill health. A young man suffered a disappointment in love which sent him to a hospital. For months he hovered between life and death. A specialist in suggestive therapeutics was called in. The specialist changed nurses, placing him in charge of a very charming young woman who began (by pre-arrangement with the doctor) to make love to him the first day of her arrival on the job. Within three weeks the patient was discharged from the hospital, still suffering, but with an entirely different malady. HE WAS IN LOVE AGAIN. The remedy was a hoax, but the patient and the nurse were later married.

SYMPTOMS OF THE FEAR OF ILL HEALTH

The symptoms of this almost universal fear are:

❑ AUTO-SUGGESTION. The habit of negative use of self-suggestion by looking for, and expecting to find the symptoms of all kinds of disease.

❑ HYPOCHONDRIA. The habit of talking of illness, concentrating the mind upon disease, and expecting its appearance until a nervous break occurs. This condition is brought on by negative thinking and nothing but positive thought can affect a cure.

❑ SUSCEPTIBILITY. Fear of ill health breaks down Nature's body resistance, and creates a favorable condition for any form of disease one may contact. The fear of ill health often is related to the fear of Poverty, especially in the case of the hypochondriac, who constantly worries about the possibility of having to pay doctor's bills, hospital bills, etc.

❑ SELF-CODDLING. The habit of making a bid for sympathy, using imaginary illness as the lure. (People often resort to this trick to avoid work). The habit of feigning illness to cover plain laziness, or to serve as an alibi for lack of ambition.

❑ INTEMPERANCE. The habit of using alcohol or narcotics to destroy pains such as headaches, neuralgia, etc., instead of eliminating the cause.

THE FEAR OF LOSS OF LOVE

The original source of this inherent fear needs but little description, because it obviously grew out of man's polygamous habit of stealing his fellow-man's mate, and his habit of taking liberties with her whenever he could. Jealousy grows out of man's inherited fear of the loss of love of someone.

This fear is the most painful of all the six basic fears. It probably plays more havoc with the body and mind than any of the other basic fears, as it sometimes leads to permanent insanity.

SYMPTOMS OF THE FEAR OF LOSS OF LOVE

❑ JEALOUSY. The habit of being suspicious of friends and loved ones without any reasonable evidence of sufficient grounds. General suspicion of everyone, absolute faith in no one.

❑ FAULT FINDING. The habit of finding fault with friends, relatives, business associates and loved ones upon the slightest provocation, or without any cause whatsoever.

❑ GAMBLING. The habit of gambling, stealing, cheating, and otherwise taking hazardous chances to provide money for loved ones, with the belief that love can be bought. The habit of spending beyond one's means, or incurring debts, to provide gifts for loved ones, with the object of making a favorable showing. Insomnia, nervousness, lack of persistence, weakness of will, lack of self-control, lack of self-reliance, bad temper.

Note: This description of the fear of loss of love is incomplete: the source of this fear is not revealed. We come into this world expecting and generally getting love the first months of our life, whereupon love is starting to fade, giving place to the individuation process. Some people are fortunate to have been cared for by loving parents, siblings and relatives, and they develop healthy and loving relationships with friends and partners, but these are relatively rare. Most people do have experiences telling them that the love they need does not live long, and once found a friend or a partner, they might cling to them, or push them away, in fear of losing them one day and being badly hurt. Fear never leads to benefit – or to love. Whatever the experiences, it is important to connect to the loving force of the "ether" as the author calls the unified field, and stay safe in loving relationships.

THE FEAR OF OLD AGE

In the main, this fear grows out of two sources. First, the thought that old age may bring with it POVERTY. Secondly, and by far the most common source of origin, from false and cruel teachings of the past.

The possibility of ill health, which is more common as people grow older, is also a contributing cause of this common fear of old age. Eroticism also enters into the cause of the fear of old age, as no man cherishes the thought of diminishing sex attraction.

Another contributing cause of the fear of old age, is the possibility of loss of freedom and independence, as old age may bring with it the loss of both physical and economic freedom.

Note: many businesses thrive on people's fears, and fear of old age and loss of attractiveness in particular.

SYMPTOMS OF THE FEAR OF OLD AGE

❑ The tendency to slow down and develop an inferiority complex at the age of mental maturity, around the age of forty, falsely believing one's self to be "slipping" because of age. (The truth is that man's most useful years, mentally and spiritually, are those between forty and sixty).

❑ The habit of speaking apologetically of one's self as "being old" merely because one has reached the age of forty, or fifty, instead of reversing the rule and expressing gratitude for having reached the age of wisdom and understanding.

❑ The habit of killing off initiative, imagination, and self-reliance by falsely believing one's self too old to exercise these qualities. The habit of the man or woman of forty dressing with the aim of trying to appear much younger, and affecting mannerisms of youth; thereby inspiring ridicule by both friends and strangers.

THE FEAR OF DEATH

To some this is the cruelest of all the basic fears. "Come into my tent, embrace my faith, accept my dogmas, and I will give you a ticket that will admit you straightaway into heaven when you die," cries a leader of sectarianism. "Remain out of my tent," says the same leader, "and may the devil take you and burn you throughout eternity." ETERNITY is a long time. FIRE is a terrible thing. The thought of eternal punishment, with fire, not only causes man to fear death, it often causes him to lose his reason. It destroys interest in life and makes happiness impossible.

During my research, I reviewed a book entitled "A Catalogue of the Gods," in which were listed the 30,000 gods which man has worshiped. Think of it! Thirty thousand of them, represented by everything from a crawfish to a man. It is little wonder that men have become frightened at the approach of death.

While the religious leader may not be able to provide safe conduct into heaven, nor, by lack of such provision, allow the unfortunate to descend into hell, the possibility of the latter seems so terrible that the very thought of it lays hold of the imagination in such a realistic way that it paralyzes reason, and sets up the fear of death.

In truth, NO MAN KNOWS, and no man has ever known, what heaven or hell is like, nor does any man know if either place actually exists. This very lack of positive knowledge opens the door of the human mind to the charlatan so he may enter and control that mind with his stock of legerdemain and various brands of pious fraud and trickery.

The fear of DEATH is not as common now as it was during the age when there were no great colleges and universities. Through the aid of biology, astronomy, geology, and other related sciences, the fears of the dark ages which gripped the minds of men and destroyed their reason have been dispelled.

This fear is useless. Death will come, no matter what anyone may think about it. Accept it as a necessity, and pass the thought out of your mind. It must be a, necessity, or it would not come to all. Perhaps it is not as bad as it has been pictured.

The entire world is made up of only two things, ENERGY and MATTER. In elementary physics we learn that neither matter nor energy (the only two realities known to man) can be created nor destroyed. Both matter and energy can be transformed, but neither can be destroyed.

Life is energy, if it is anything. If neither energy nor matter can be destroyed, of course life cannot be destroyed. Life, like other forms of energy, may be passed through various processes of transition, or change, but it cannot be destroyed. Death is mere transition.

If death is not mere change, or transition, then nothing comes after death except a long, eternal, peaceful sleep, and sleep is nothing to be feared. Thus you may wipe out, forever, the fear of Death.

SYMPTOMS OF THE FEAR OF DEATH

The habit of THINKING about dying instead of making the most of LIFE, is due, generally, to lack of purpose, or lack of a suitable occupation. This fear is more prevalent among the aged, but sometimes the more youthful are victims of it. The greatest of all remedies for the fear of death is a BURNING DESIRE FOR ACHIEVEMENT, backed by useful service to others. Happy people seldom have time to think about dying. They find life too thrilling to worry about death. Sometimes the fear of death is closely associated with the Fear of Poverty, where one's death would leave loved ones poverty-stricken. In other cases, the fear of death is caused by illness and the consequent breaking down of physical body resistance. The commonest causes of the fear of death are: ill-health, poverty, lack of appropriate occupation, disappointment over love, insanity, religious fanaticism.

WORRY

Worry is a state of mind based upon fear. It works slowly, but persistently. It is insidious and subtle. Step by step it "digs itself in" until it paralyzes one's reasoning faculty, destroys self-confidence and initiative. Worry is a form of sustained fear caused by indecision therefore it is a state of mind which can be controlled.

An unsettled mind is helpless. Indecision makes an unsettled mind. Most individuals lack the willpower to reach decisions promptly, and to stand by them after they have been made, even during normal business conditions. During periods of economic unrest, the individual is handicapped, not alone by his inherent nature to be slow at reaching decisions, but he is influenced by the indecision of others around him who have created a state of "mass indecision."

"Fearenza" and "Worryitis" are the two mental disease germs. There is only one known antidote for these germs; it is the habit of prompt and firm DECISION. Moreover, it is an antidote which every individual must apply for himself.

We do not worry over conditions, once we have reached a decision to follow a definite line of action. Decision can induce change of undesired circumstances.

The six basic fears become translated into a state of worry, through indecision.

Whip the fear of poverty by reaching a decision to get along with whatever wealth you can accumulate WITHOUT WORRY.

Put your foot upon the neck of the fear of criticism by reaching a decision NOT TO WORRY about what other people think, do, or say.

Kill the habit of worry, in all its forms, by reaching a general, blanket decision that nothing which life has to offer is worth the price of worry. With this decision will come poise, peace of mind, and calmness of thought which will bring happiness.

A man whose mind is filled with fear not only destroys his own chances of intelligent action, but, he transmits these destructive vibrations to the minds of all who come into contact with him, and destroys, also their chances.

Even a dog or a horse knows when its master lacks courage; moreover, a dog or a horse will pick up the vibrations of fear thrown off by its master, and behave accordingly. Lower down the line of intelligence in the animal kingdom, one finds this same capacity to pick up the vibrations of fear. A honey-bee immediately senses fear in the mind of a person—for reasons unknown, a bee will sting the person whose mind is releasing vibrations of fear, much more readily than it will molest the person whose mind registers no fear.

The vibrations of fear pass from one mind to another just as quickly and as surely as the sound of the human voice passes from the broadcasting station to the receiving set of a radio—and by similar medium.

Mental telepathy is a reality. Thoughts pass from one mind to another, voluntarily, whether or not this fact is recognized by either the person releasing the thoughts, or the persons who pick up those thoughts.

The person who gives expression to negative or destructive thoughts is practically certain to experience the results of those words in the form of a destructive "kickback." The release of destructive thought impulses, alone, without the aid of words, produces also a "kickback" in more ways than one. First of all, and perhaps most important to be remembered, the person who releases thoughts of a destructive nature, must suffer damage through the breaking down of the faculty of creative imagination. Secondly, the presence in the mind of any destructive emotion develops a negative personality which repels people, and often converts them into antagonists. The third source of damage to the person who entertains or releases negative thoughts, lies in this significant fact—these thought-impulses are not only damaging to others, but they IMBED THEMSELVES IN THE SUBCONSCIOUS MIND OF THE PERSON RELEASING THEM, and there become a part of his character.

One is never through with a thought, merely by releasing it. When a thought is released, it spreads in every direction, through the medium of the ether, but it also plants itself permanently in the subconscious mind of the person releasing it.

Note: Stop every unfavorable thought or give it a reshape right at the moment of releasing. Reframe techniques, humor, your basic good nature, joy, love and wishing well to everyone are your aids in this endeavor.

Your business in life is presumably to achieve success. To be successful, you must find peace of mind, acquire the material needs of life, and above all, attain HAPPINESS. All of these evidences of success begin in the form of thought impulses.

You may control your own mind, you have the power to feed it whatever thought impulses you choose. With this privilege goes also the responsibility of using it constructively. You are the master of your own earthly destiny just as surely as you have the power to control your own thoughts. You may influence, direct, and eventually control your own environment, making your life what you want it to be—or, you may neglect to exercise the privilege which is yours, to make your life to order, thus casting yourself upon the broad sea of "Circumstance" where you will be tossed hither and yon, like a chip on the waves of the ocean.

THE SEVENTH BASIC EVIL

In addition to the Six Basic Fears, there is another evil by which people suffer. It constitutes a rich soil in which the seeds of failure grow abundantly. It is so subtle that its presence often is not detected.

This affliction cannot properly be classed as a fear. IT IS MORE DEEPLY SEATED AND MORE OFTEN FATAL THAN ALL OF THE SIX FEARS. For want of a better name, let us call this evil **SUSCEPTIBILITY TO NEGATIVE INFLUENCES**.

Men who accumulate great riches always protect themselves against this evil! The poverty stricken never do! Those who succeed in any calling must prepare their minds to resist the evil. If you are reading this philosophy for the purpose of accumulating riches or attaining happiness, you should examine yourself very carefully, to determine whether you are susceptible to negative influences. If you neglect this self-analysis, you will forfeit your right to attain the object of your desires.

Make the analysis searching. After you read the questions prepared for this self-analysis, hold yourself to a strict accounting in your answers. Go at the task as carefully as you would search for any other enemy you knew to be awaiting you in ambush and deal with your own faults as you would with a more tangible enemy.

You can easily protect yourself against highway robbers, because the law provides organized cooperation for your benefit, but the "seventh basic evil" is more difficult to master, because it strikes when you are not aware of its presence, when you are asleep, and while you are awake. Moreover, its weapon is intangible, because it consists of merely—a STATE OF MIND. This evil is also dangerous because it strikes in as many different forms as there are human experiences. Sometimes it enters the mind through the well-meant words of one's own relatives. At other times, it bores from within, through one's own mental attitude. Always it is as deadly as poison, even though it may not kill as quickly.

HOW TO PROTECT YOURSELF AGAINST NEGATIVE INFLUENCES

To protect yourself against negative influences, whether of your own making, or the result of the activities or negative thoughts of people around you, recognize that you have a WILL-POWER, and put it into constant use, until it builds a wall of immunity against negative influences in your own mind.

Recognize if you are, by nature, lazy, indifferent, and susceptible to all suggestions which harmonize with your weaknesses. Recognize if you are, by nature, susceptible to all the six basic fears, and set up habits for the purpose of counteracting all these fears.

Recognize that negative influences often work on you through your subconscious mind, therefore they are difficult to detect, and keep your mind closed against all people who depress or discourage you in any way.

Deliberately seek the company of people who influence you to THINK AND ACT FOR YOURSELF. Do not EXPECT troubles.

Without doubt, the most common weakness of all human beings is the habit of **leaving their minds open to the negative influence of other people**. This weakness is all the more damaging, because most people do not recognize that they are cursed by it, and many who acknowledge it, neglect or refuse to correct the evil until it becomes an uncontrollable part of their daily habits.

To aid those who wish to see themselves as they really are, the following list of questions has been prepared. Read the questions and state your answers aloud, so you can hear your own voice. This will make it easier for you to be truthful with yourself.

SELF-ANALYSIS TEST QUESTIONS

❑ Do you complain often of "feeling bad," and if so, what is the cause?

❑ Do you find fault with other people at the slightest provocation?

❑ Do you frequently make mistakes in your work, and if so, why?

❑ Are you sarcastic and offensive in your conversation?

❑ Do you deliberately avoid the association of anyone, and if so, why?

- Do you suffer frequently with indigestion? If so, what is the cause?
- Does life seem futile and the future hopeless to you? If so, why?
- Do you like your occupation? If not, why?
- Do you often feel self-pity, and if so why?
- Are you envious of those who excel you?
- To which do you devote most time, thinking of SUCCESS, or of FAILURE?
- Are you gaining or losing self-confidence as you grow older?
- Do you learn something of value from all mistakes?
- **Are you permitting some relative or acquaintance to worry you**? If so, why?
- Are you sometimes "in the clouds" and at other times in the depths of despondency?
- Who has the most inspiring influence upon you? What is the cause?
- Do you tolerate negative or discouraging influences which you can avoid?
- Are you careless of your personal appearance? If so, when and why?
- Have you learned how to "drown your troubles" by being too busy to be annoyed by them?
- Would you call yourself a "spineless weakling" if you permitted others to do your thinking for you?
- Do you neglect internal bathing until auto-intoxication makes you ill-tempered and irritable?
- How many preventable disturbances annoy you, and why do you tolerate them?
- Do you resort to liquor, narcotics, or cigarettes to "quiet your nerves"? If so, why do you not try will-power instead?
- Does anyone "nag" you, and if so, for what reason?
- Do you have a DEFINITE MAJOR PURPOSE, and if so, what is it, and what plan have you for achieving it?
- Do you suffer from any of the Six Basic Fears? If so, which ones?
- Have you a method by which you can shield yourself against the negative influence of others?

- Do you make deliberate use of auto-suggestion to make your mind positive?
- Which do you value most, your material possessions, or your privilege of controlling your own thoughts?
- Are you easily influenced by others, against your own judgment?
- Has today added anything of value to your stock of knowledge or state of mind?
- Do you face squarely the circumstances which make you unhappy, or sidestep the responsibility?
- Do you analyze all mistakes and failures and try to profit by them or, do you take the attitude that this is not your duty?
- Can you name three of your most damaging weaknesses? What are you doing to correct them?
- Do you encourage other people to bring their worries to you for sympathy?
- Do you choose, from your daily experiences, lessons or influences which aid in your personal advancement?
- Does your presence have a negative influence on other people as a rule?
- What habits of other people annoy you most?
- Do you form your own opinions or permit yourself to be influenced by other people?
- Have you learned how to create a mental state of mind with which you can shield yourself against all discouraging influences?
- Does your occupation inspire you with faith and hope?
- Are you conscious of possessing spiritual forces of sufficient power to enable you to keep your mind free from all forms of FEAR?
- Does your religion help you to keep your own mind positive?
- Do you feel it your duty to share other people's worries? If so, why?
- If you believe that "birds of a feather flock together" what have you learned about yourself by studying the friends whom you attract?

- What connection, if any, do you see between the people with whom you associate most closely, and any unhappiness you may experience?
- Could it be possible that some person whom you consider to be a friend is, in reality, your worst enemy, because of his negative influence on your mind?
- By what rules do you judge who is helpful and who is damaging to you?
- Are your intimate associates mentally superior or inferior to you?
- How much time out of every 24 hours do you devote to:
  - your occupation
  - sleep
  - play and relaxation
  - acquiring useful knowledge
  - plain waste
- Who among your acquaintances,
  - encourages you most
  - cautions you most
  - discourages you most
  - helps you most in other ways
- What is your greatest worry? Why do you tolerate it?
- When others offer you free, unsolicited advice, do you accept it without question, or analyze their motive?
- What, above all else, do you most DESIRE? Do you intend to acquire or attain it?
- Are you willing to subordinate all other desires for this one?
- How much time daily do you devote to it?
- Do you change your mind often? If so, why?
- Do you usually finish everything you begin?
- Are you easily impressed by other people's business or professional titles, college degrees, or wealth?
- Are you easily influenced by what other people think or say of you?
- Do you cater to people because of their social or financial status?

❑ Whom do you believe to be the greatest person living? In what respect is this person superior to yourself?

How much time have you devoted to studying and answering these questions? (At least one day is necessary for the analysis and the answering of the entire list).

If you have answered all these questions truthfully, you know more about yourself than the majority of people. Study the questions carefully, come back to them once each week for several months, and be astounded at the amount of additional knowledge of great value to yourself, you will have gained by the simple method of answering the questions truthfully. If you are not certain concerning the answers to some of the questions, seek the counsel of those who know you well, especially those who have no motive in flattering you, and see yourself through their eyes. The experience will be astonishing.

You have ABSOLUTE CONTROL over but one thing, and that is your thoughts. This is the most significant and inspiring of all facts known to man! It reflects man's Divine nature. This Divine prerogative is the sole means by which you may control your own destiny. If you fail to control your own mind, you may be sure you will control nothing else.

If you must be careless with your possessions, let it be in connection with material things. Your mind is your spiritual estate! Protect and use it with the care to which Divine Royalty is entitled. You were given a WILL-POWER for this purpose.

Unfortunately, there is no legal protection against those who, either by design or ignorance, poison the minds of others by negative suggestion. This form of destruction should be punishable by heavy legal penalties, because it may and often does destroy one's chances of acquiring material things which are protected by law.

The mind could produce ANYTHING THE MIND COULD CONCEIVE AND BELIEVE. This knowledge is the thing that will lift you above the common herd.

Mind control is the result of self-discipline and habit. You either control your mind or it controls you. There is no hall-way compromise. The most practical of all methods for controlling the mind is the habit of keeping it busy with a definite purpose, backed by a definite plan.

"FIFTY-SEVEN" FAMOUS ALIBIS

People who do not succeed have one distinguishing trait in common. They know all the reasons for failure, and have what they believe to be air-tight alibis to explain away their own lack of achievement. Some of these alibis are clever, and a few of them are justifiable by the facts. But alibis cannot be used for money. The world wants to know only one thing—HAVE YOU ACHIEVED SUCCESS?

A character analyst compiled a list of the most commonly used alibis. As you read the list, examine yourself carefully, and determine how many of these alibis, if any, are your own property. Remember, too, the philosophy presented in this book makes every one of these alibis obsolete.

- ❑ IF I didn't have a wife and family. . .
- ❑ IF I had enough "pull" . . .
- ❑ IF I had money . . .
- ❑ IF I had a good education . . .
- ❑ IF I could get a job . . .
- ❑ IF I had good health . . .
- ❑ IF I only had time . . .
- ❑ IF times were better . . .
- ❑ IF other people understood me . . .
- ❑ IF conditions around me were only different . . .
- ❑ IF I could live my life over again . . .
- ❑ IF I did not fear what "THEY" would say . . .
- ❑ IF I had been given a chance . . .
- ❑ IF I now had a chance . . .
- ❑ IF other people didn't "have it in for me" . . .
- ❑ IF nothing happens to stop me . . .

- ❑ IF I were only younger . . .
- ❑ IF I could only do what I want . . .
- ❑ IF I had been born rich . . .
- ❑ IF I could meet "the right people" . . .
- ❑ IF I had the talent that some people have . . .
- ❑ IF I dared assert myself . . .
- ❑ IF I only had embraced past opportunities . . .
- ❑ IF people didn't get on my nerves . . .
- ❑ IF I didn't have to keep house and look after the children . . .
- ❑ IF I could save some money . . .
- ❑ IF the boss only appreciated me . . .
- ❑ IF I only had somebody to help me . . .
- ❑ IF my family understood me . . .
- ❑ IF I lived in a big city . . .
- ❑ IF I could just get started . . .
- ❑ IF I were only free . . .
- ❑ IF I had the personality of some people . . .
- ❑ IF I were not so fat . . .
- ❑ IF my talents were known . . .
- ❑ IF I could just get a "break" . . .
- ❑ IF I could only get out of debt . . .
- ❑ IF I hadn't failed . . .
- ❑ IF I only knew how . . .
- ❑ IF everybody didn't oppose me . . .
- ❑ IF I didn't have so many worries . . .
- ❑ IF I could marry the right person . . .
- ❑ IF people weren't so dumb . . .
- ❑ IF my family were not so extravagant . . .
- ❑ IF I were sure of myself . . .
- ❑ IF luck were not against me . . .
- ❑ IF I had not been born under the wrong star . . .
- ❑ IF it were not true that "what is to be will be" . . .
- ❑ IF I did not have to work so hard . . .
- ❑ IF I hadn't lost my money . . .
- ❑ IF I lived in a different neighborhood . . .

- ❑ IF I didn't have a "past" . . .
- ❑ IF I only had a business of my own . . .
- ❑ IF other people would only listen to me . . .

IF – and this is the greatest of them all – I had the courage to see myself as I really am, I would find out what is wrong with me, and correct it, then I might have a chance to profit by my mistakes and learn something from the experience of others, for I know that there is something WRONG with me, or I would now be where I WOULD HAVE BEEN IF I had spent more time analyzing my weaknesses, and less time building alibis to cover them.

Building alibis with which to explain away failure is a national pastime. The habit is as old as the human race, and is fatal to success! Why do people cling to their pet alibis? The answer is obvious. They defend their alibis because THEY CREATE them! A man's alibi is the child of his own imagination. It is human nature to defend one's own brain-child.

Building alibis is a deeply rooted habit. Habits are difficult to break, especially when they provide justification for something we do. Plato had this truth in mind when he said, "The first and best victory is to conquer self. To be conquered by self is, of all things, the most shameful and vile."

Another philosopher had the same thought in mind when he said, "It was a great surprise to me when I discovered that most of the ugliness I saw in others, was but a reflection of my own nature."

Note: If you meet, say, a dishonest person or a coward, and call them so in your mind, they are not necessarily a reflection of your own nature. Gregg Braden in his book "The Divine Matrix", describes another type, the "second mirror", which mirrors what we JUDGE, not what we ARE. Dealing with own judgments is the second step in building one's character after dealing with own faults, reflected by other people in one's life.

"It has always been a mystery to me," said Elbert Hubbard, "why people spend so much time deliberately fooling themselves by creating alibis to cover their weaknesses. If used differently, this same time would be sufficient to cure the weakness, then no alibis would be needed."

In parting, I would remind you that "Life is a checkerboard, and the player opposite you is TIME. If you hesitate before moving, or neglect to move promptly, your men will be wiped off the board by TIME. You are playing against a partner who will not tolerate INDECISION!"

Previously you may have had a logical excuse for not having forced Life to come through with whatever you asked, but that alibi is now obsolete, because you are in possession of the Master Key that unlocks the door to Life's bountiful riches.

The Master Key is intangible, but it is powerful! It is the privilege of creating, in your own mind, a BURNING DESIRE for a definite form of riches. There is no penalty for the use of the Key, but there is a price you must pay if you do not use it. The price is FAILURE. There is a reward of stupendous proportions if you put the Key to use. It is the satisfaction that comes to all who conquer self and force Life to pay whatever is asked.

The reward is worthy of your effort. Will you make the start and be convinced?

"If we are related," said the immortal Emerson, "we shall meet." In closing, may I borrow his thought, and say, "If we are related, we have, through these pages, met."

THE END

CPSIA information can be obtained
at www.ICGtesting.com
Printed in the USA
BVHW011148190821
614774BV00016B/321